Community, Democracy, and the Environment

HARRY C. TREXLER
LIBRARY

Compliments of

Tammy Lewis

Reviews Editor of

Society & Natural

Resources

Community, Democracy, and the Environment

Learning to Share the Future

Jane A. Grant

ROWMAN & LITTLEFIELD PUBLISHERS, INC.
Lanham • Boulder • New York • Toronto • Oxford

ROWMAN & LITTLEFIELD PUBLISHERS, INC.

Published in the United States of America
by Rowman & Littlefield Publishers, Inc.
A wholly owned subsidiary of The Rowman & Littlefield Publishing Group, Inc.
4501 Forbes Boulevard, Suite 200, Lanham, Maryland 20706
www.rowmanlittlefield.com

PO Box 317
Oxford
OX2 9RU, UK

British Library Cataloguing in Publication Information Available

Library of Congress Cataloging-in-Publication Data

Grant, Jane A.
    Community, democracy, and the environment: learning to share the
future / Jane A. Grant.
        p.   cm.
    Includes bibliographical references and index.
    ISBN 0-7425-2614-3 (alk. paper) – ISBN 0-7425-2615-1 (pbk.: alk. paper)
    1. Sustainable development—United States.   2. Environmental policy—
United States—Citizen participation.   3. Energy policy—United States.
4. Political ethics—United States.   5. Social values—United States.
6. Common good.   I. Title.
    HC110.E5G716   2003
    338.973'07—dc21   2003010702

Printed in the United States of America

∞ ™ The paper used in this publication meets the minimum requirements of
American National Standard for Information Sciences—Permanence of Paper for
Printed Library Materials, ANSI/NISO Z39.48-1992.

To Anna and Samuel Ostrow and Jennie and Charles Zoosie-Grant,
my grandparents,
who took the risk to come to America,
and to my father, Martin Grant,
who loved many things American

Contents

Acknowledgments   ix

1   Community, Democracy, and the Environment: Overview and Background   1

2   Discussion, Participation, Deliberation, and Modern Community: Connections with Public Spheres, Governmental Sectors, Civil Ethics, and Environmental Values   17

3   Fostering Democratic Deliberation over Environmental Policy: The Indiana Hazardous Waste Facility Site Approval Authority   41

4   The Environment, Energy Policy, and Sustainable Development in the United States: Historical Antecedents and Future Prospects   67

5   Global Climate Change: Linking National Deliberations with International Negotiations   91

6   Conclusion: Learning to Share the Future   109

Index   125

About the Author   135

Acknowledgments

I want to thank Jane Marie Silva, for her loving support, decency, compassion, commitment to moral principles, and embrace of life. I am grateful as well to the other members of my family who have provided me with support, encouragement, and love throughout my life, especially my mother, Loretta Grant; my sister, Susan C. Glanz; my aunt, Mina Ostrow; my uncle, Sol Ostrow; my cousin, Leonard Gornstein; and my "aunt," Geneva Listenberger. Among them I have learned to be fully myself, yet irrevocably linked to a circle of caring, humor, and integrity. With them, I have come to understand the meaning of the "middle way."

My appreciation also extends to my colleagues at Indiana University–Purdue University, Fort Wayne, who have provided me with encouragement and support, as well as camaraderie and friendship over the years. They include Bill Ludwin, Brian Fife, Tom Guthrie, Mike Nusbaumer, and Tammy Davich. I also wish to thank Valerie Richardson for her invaluable research assistance and Kirsten Gronbjerg, at Indiana University, Bloomington, for her invaluable advice on publishing. Some colleagues from graduate school have remained good friends over the years, and they continue to provide me with inspiration, especially Kathleen Gerson, John Mollenkopf, and Rob Mayer. Margaret Wilder has also been both a great friend and colleague. There are also a number of individuals in Fort Wayne whom I have come to know, respect, and develop great affection for over the years I studied the developments around the Adams Center Landfill. I especially want to thank Cheryl Hitzemann, Jim Fenton, Alan ver Planck, Bob and Joan Beineke, and Tom Lewandowski. Friends who have helped to provide balance in my life and to whom I am deeply grateful include Judy Fors, Sue Augustus, Sandy Manheimer, Jeff Markley, Kenton Neuhouser, Laura Stine, Tessa Gochtovtt, Belinda Planck, Teresa Cage, Mo and Tom Palmer, and Tom Webb.

For additional uncompromising support, I want to thank the other beings who share our household, especially Shayna Mabel, Muriel, and

Mattie and the memories of Dahlia, Emma Golden, Earl, and Clelia. My sincere appreciation goes to Billie and the staff at Keltsch's, who saved the *New York Times* for me every day. I also derive immense inspiration from the life and work of Hannah Arendt, Emile Durkheim, Robert Bellah, Jane Mansbridge, Lynton K. Caldwell, Jimmy Carter, and the Dalai Lama. I am indebted to the music of Rodgers and Hammerstein, Pete Seeger, the Robert Shaw Chorale, and countless others who have provided me with deep joy and a sense of sharing in a common journey through their creations. I would like to thank the many students in my classes over the years who have blessed me with their desire to learn and the opportunity to participate in that process. Finally, I wish to thank Brian Romer, field publisher at Rowman & Littlefield, whose enterprising spirit, can-do attitude, and commitment to excellence I very much appreciate; Hedi Hong, assistant editor, and the staff at Rowman & Littlefield, for their very helpful assistance; and the anonymous reviewers, whose thoughtful comments not only improved the text, but exemplify the best of the "discourse" model of society.

1

Community, Democracy, and the Environment: Overview and Background

One song America, before I go,
I'd sing o'er all the rest, with trumpet sound,
For thee—the Future.

—Walt Whitman, "One Song America before I Go"

OVERVIEW

Ensuring the continued integrity of the global environment may now be linked to the ability of humans to strengthen existing, and develop new, opportunities and institutions in which to democratically explore policies, goals, and ethics affecting the future. While it may not seem obvious, the nature of the ties we have to one another in our communities, the quality of the attachments we have to our political institutions, and the presence or absence of public spaces within which to deliberate about our deepest concerns may have profound implications for the biosphere. At least, that is the argument of this book. The first two chapters explore the changing character of community and the polity in the United States and suggest what the significance of those transformations might be for environmental politics, policy, and ideals. Community, in its most general sense, connotes the type of ties that bind citizens to one another and to values that may shape their lives, provide meaning to their existence, and set limits on their behavior. Our relationship to critical decision-making institutions and the kind of citizenship it promotes can be said to typ-

1

ify our polity, or societal governance structures. The apparent loosening
of communal connections and weakening of civic configurations in
America have occurred for a number of historical, social, political, and
economic reasons, since the nation's founding.[1] While resulting in significant benefits, including increased freedom for individuals to pursue
their own notions of happiness, increased equality among population
groups, and increased attention to institutional fairness and equal protection of the laws, these changes have also had their costs. Citizens now
seem intently focused on their own self-interests, with less concern for
what might be called the common good. Developing shared principles to
help direct our associations with each other, with other nations, and with
the variety of species and ecosystems on the earth seems to garner little
attention. Chapter 1 provides some background on the contemporary
dynamics of environmental politics and policy in the United States and
the role that the concept of sustainable development may play in reconcil-
ing conflicting outlooks on environmental protection; these themes are
also explored in chapters 4, 5, and 6.

Chapter 2 then examines the types of processes, institutions, and values
that might increase the avenues for citizens to discuss, participate in, and
deliberate over environmental programs and policies, as well as help in
creating a realm of civil ethics. This latter sphere could provide a public
locus for democratically considering the ideals we think are important to
our future. Civil ethics may be useful in a number of areas, but none more
than the global environment. The biosphere is shaped by a set of principles, including that of limits and interconnectedness. There is ultimately
a finite amount of resources on the earth (even those that are potentially
renewable can be overused), and there is a finite ability of the earth to
absorb the waste products from our systems of production and consumption. Something added to or removed from one ecosystem can have profound implications for all the rest.[2] So if ethics have something to do with
limits and responsibilities, then it seems there would be a critical role for
them in decisions about the environment.[3] Increased discussion of, participation in, and deliberation over environmental goals, and new paths for
developing the realm of civil ethics, may need to be guided by the notion
of the "middle way."[4] The middle way in policy deliberations requires
remaining open to a wide range of options, developing some understanding of the common good, yet also being cognizant of the limits beyond
which participants in the discussion can no longer in good faith agree.[5]
The middle way in creating a civil ethos refers to the effort to ground such
an undertaking between the extremes of deeply held private beliefs and
the vacuum of contemporary shared public beliefs. Here especially, one
would have to recognize the point at which "disagreements become nondeliberative," such that individuals' own moral or ethical commitments

prevent them from being able to endorse a particular policy approach or civil ethics component.[6] This concept is broached in chapter 2, but more fully examined in chapter 6. The realm of civil ethics may provide us with a site in which to develop principles to guide relationships critical to our future, including those with fellow citizens, future generations, other nations, and other species.

Chapter 3 turns to an actual deliberation over the location of a hazardous waste landfill in the Midwest, an issue that engulfed a community for three decades. The location of hazardous waste facilities dominated the national environmental policy agenda, especially in the 1980s.[7] This case study scrutinizes a deliberation process that helped to extract a publicly oriented and equitable resolution out of a highly polarized policy conflict. Although the deliberative mechanism never focused explicitly on "foundational" environmental values,[8] it used fairness and a search for the commonweal as its signposts. It thus may provide one model for deliberating over environmental programs and policies in the public sphere and governmental sectors.[9] Chapter 4 turns to an environmental policy issue that emerged in the first decade of the modern environmental movement in the United States and is still at the forefront of the nation's environmental policy debate: the direction of energy policy. The chapter reviews the changing orientations of Americans to the environment and environmental policy throughout our history, and examines why the topic of energy policy has proven so contentious and seemingly intractable, yet so critical to our environmental future. Chapter 5 links energy policy to one of the key global environmental problems now facing the planet: climate change. The chapter looks at the role of energy choices in global climate warming, examines our current unwillingness to join with other nations to address this key global environmental issue, and proposes the development of processes and institutions at the local, state, and national levels that could provide occasions to discuss, participate in, and deliberate about our energy future and link these activities to ongoing international negotiations about global warming. Chapter 6 appraises the advantages and disadvantages of seeking more discussion of, participation in, and deliberation about environmental programs, policies, and goals and enhancing the realm of biospheric ethics in the United States. It also examines how the notion of sustainable development may provide a vital connection for learning to share the future with each other, and with all the other beings with whom we share the planet.

BACKGROUND: THE CHANGING NATURE OF COMMUNITY AND THE POLITY IN AMERICA

Social and political theorists have long been concerned with the changing nature of both community and the polity in modern industrialized socie-

ties. Since the end of the nineteenth century, the transition from gemeinschaft (community) to gesellschaft (society)[10] has been a central concern
for sociologists. Emile Durkheim (1858–1917) explored the question of
what would or could replace the thick ties of affection and solidarity that
bound persons together in groups in preindustrial societies. Modern
industrial societies, undergoing a division of labor characterized by distinct spheres of state and society, and by vast specialization within, have
exhibited evidence of weakened social integration, increased individua-
tion, and the seeming loss of commitment to or concern about the common good. Durkheim and other social theorists since have wondered
where the new loci for the development of shared beliefs and practices to
protect us from the modern fates of alienation, anxiety, and apathy would
be located.[11]

Political scientists have also been concerned about attenuating civic
relationships, particularly with the decline of the all-encompassing polity.[12] The unitary system of democracy practiced in early Greece—as well
as the earliest hunting and gathering societies, the assemblies of the
ninth-century Vikings, and the republics of medieval and Renaissance
Italy—exemplified an understanding that even protracted political
debates may yield to the discovery of underlying common interests and
that face-to-face deliberations could play a central role in revealing new
understandings of old subjects.[13] Hannah Arendt argued that this early
model of democracy held *transformative* possibilities: people meeting in a
public setting, listening and responding to the ideas, beliefs, and values
of others, might potentially arrive at new, even unforeseen insights.[14] She
recognized, of course, that this early polity was in fact exclusionary, deny-
ing access to it by non–property holders, slaves, women, and others not
designated as citizens. She also understood that the transition from a
ubiquitous and relatively homogeneous polity, in which virtue and cour-
age were prized, to a contracted public space, as state and society became
distinct in modern societies, would pose a challenge to meaningful deliberation in social systems that were becoming increasingly heterogeneous
and inclusive.[15]

Michael Sandel[16] analyzes the American transition from a civic republic
to a procedural republic. Civic republicanism was the more dominant orientation in the founding and during the first century of the country's creation; it has been on the decline, Sandel argues, since the early twentieth
century. Civic republicanism emphasizes a shared set of values and the
need for a polity to shape individuals so that they are capable of participating in their own self-governance. This political philosophy was not
limited to the institutions of government, but was a set of beliefs that
influenced schools, workplaces, and the organizations of an emergent
civil society. The American civic republic, like the earlier Greek and later

Roman republics, however, was characterized by an exclusivity that perhaps made it easier for shared ideals to develop. Robert Bellah[17] suggests that there were three cultural sources members of the early American polity drew upon that encouraged them to see their fates as shared: the republican idea of civic virtue, the Old Testament belief in a Covenant between humans and God, and the New Testament understanding of a community established through love and fellowship.

It may be argued that it was the increased demand for inclusion in the polity, beginning in the late nineteenth century and running through the mid-twentieth, by groups such as African Americans, other ethnic minorities, and women, and later, in the latter half of the twentieth century, by gays, the disabled, and still others, that helped shift the predominant orientation in the United States from a civic republic to a procedural republic. Beginning in the late 1930s, Sandel[18] believes, procedural liberalism, although present at the beginning, became the dominant political philosophy in America. This orientation stresses the singular importance of individual rights, as rights would now firmly precede any notion of the commonweal, and the state would act as the protector of these rights, showing no preference for any one comprehensive belief system. Since the diversity of beliefs may have made it impossible for any one overarching set of values to achieve general support, our political system, as James Madison had earlier promoted, would be one in which societal directions would be shaped and reshaped by the constant competition between interests. The procedural republic is firmly grounded in the liberal political philosophy of the eighteenth century.[19]

Still, observers such as Martin Marty and Bellah[20] have commented on how intertwined these two orientations have been throughout American history. While the Declaration of Independence, particularly its second paragraph, and the preamble to the Constitution contain our nation's "civic republican" ideals,[21] the Constitution itself, and the Bill of Rights that followed its ratification, emphasize the freedom of individuals to choose their own routes to the good life, relying on the voluntary sector to further these ends, while a limited government would become the fair arbiter between and the ultimate guarantor of individual rights.[22] And while Thomas Jefferson, a central figure in the writing of the Declaration, may have been influenced by Baron de Montesquieu and a civic republican notion of virtue, Madison, who was critical in the construction of the Constitution, was significantly influenced by John Locke and the liberal procedural notion of a voluntary contract among individuals—who, through social cooperation, enhance the conditions for their own liberty.[23] Bellah notes that throughout the nineteenth century, as the nation was beginning to become more diverse, certain vehicles of public culture, such as public oratory, sermons, and hymns, were able to act as fonts for shared beliefs, even as these different national philosophies contended with each other. He observes, for instance, that the "Battle Hymn of the Republic" (1862) movingly joined the civic republican orientation based on the covenant tradition and the liberal procedural one focused on individual liberty, when Julia Ward Howe wrote, "As he died to make men holy, let us die to make men free."[24]

Sandel[25] describes how, as a result of the increasing diversity of the polis, and with new demands being placed on the federal government in the 1930s, the administration of Franklin Delano Roosevelt, even with significant ties to a civic republican tradition that survived the first three decades of the twentieth century, began to shape a response to the crisis of the Depression—and later, World War II—that signaled a fuller embrace of procedural liberalism. Particularly in their reliance on Keynesian economics, Roosevelt's policies sought to maximize social welfare through the more equitable distribution of incomes to individuals and an emphasis on economic growth, without consideration of the policy impacts on individual character or civic integration.

Of course, despite the turn to procedural liberalism, issues of morality and ultimate belief systems could not be fully kept out of public discourse. As John Rawls[26] notes, however, what our system has been able to do is to create a public space where "reasonable pluralism" can exist. We may hold ultimate belief systems, and these systems may in fact influence public discussions; but reasonable pluralism requires that we explain our thinking to other citizens without having to actually reference these beliefs. This is done not only in the public sphere,[27] but in the governmental sphere as well, whether in laws emanating from the legislative realm or from executive or judicial rulings. Rawls[28] observes:

> Thus I believe that a democratic society is not and cannot be a community, where by a community I mean a body of persons united in affirming the same comprehensive, or partially comprehensive doctrine. The fact of reasonable pluralism, which characterizes a society with free institutions makes this impossible.

Still, Rawls offers two important insights about the nature of what political theorist Jürgen Habermas[29] calls the "public sphere." First, in comparison to classic liberalism, Rawls is concerned not only with the liberty of individuals to pursue their most cherished interests, but with "a public conception of justice." And second, "this public conception of justice" also provides the basis for how "citizens can adjudicate their claims of political right on their political institutions or against one another."[30] Thus, the social contract that exists among us implies reciprocity based on a shared understanding of what is just.

The public sphere is therefore social and dynamic; it changes over time as new understandings of our shared existence emerge. Chapter 2 proposes the need to develop a realm of civil ethics surrounding the public (and governmental) sphere(s), where in fact values can be addressed. Rawls believes that the most significantly held of our beliefs will remain attached to the private realm and civil society: to family, community, religious institutions, and the vast array of voluntary organizations to which Americans belong.[31] Sandel, on the other hand, worries that this tendency to place our most cherished beliefs outside of discussions in the public and governmental spheres has led to the impoverishment of these sectors, and underlies the "discontent" of contemporary democracy. He believes that not only is it almost impossible to leave these values out of our public discourse, but it is actually unwise to do so. By being explicit about our values, we may arrive at better understandings of the conflicts that engage us. Moreover, when we obscure our values, we also obscure ourselves, so that we see one another as citizens who have certain rights, rather than as full human beings with particular histories and unique characteristics. Procedural liberalism has the advantage of limiting conflict by moving the discussion of values outside of the public sphere. However, this deletion may enfeeble the public and governmental spheres, with undesirable consequences for the polity and the society.[32]

Weakened social and political ties affect attachments in civil society, nestled as it is between government and the private market. Robert D. Putnam[33] has drawn attention to what he calls the "collapse of American community." He is specifically concerned about the decrease of active involvement, during the last forty years, in the multitude of voluntary and nonprofit organizations that have characterized American civil society since the end of the nineteenth century. Analysts like Robert Wuthnow,[34] however, provide us with a different interpretation of the significance of this decline. Wuthnow agrees that our communities are more fragmented and that participation in traditional civic organizations is less robust; he also believes that the current loose network of attachments that emerged in the closing decades of the twentieth century and the opening decade of the twenty-first century accord well with the desire of Americans for greater personal freedom and new opportunities for identity formation. One could argue that the decline of the more tightly structured—but highly gendered, race-segregated, and geographically based—organizational realm created in the first half of the twentieth century was also the result of the increased demands for inclusion in the polity and society by women, African Americans, and others. Americans are now freer than ever to choose their affiliations, and analysts such as Steven Brint[35] have conceptualized a typology of modern American community that shows its immense diversity based on characteristics such as whether a community is geographically based or based on members' own proactive choices, whether it is based on shared activities or shared beliefs, and whether it requires frequent or infrequent interactions. One could argue that such freedom, if carried out by individuals who have a strong and balanced sense of who they are, may allow them to have the best of both worlds: they can pursue their own happiness by exploring and fulfilling what they have come to understand as their most important commitments, while at the same time consciously understanding that their own well-being is interconnected with the well-being of others.[36]

Sandel[37] fears that the freedom of our loosely integrated social system poses two potential dangers for citizens of the modern world. To avoid the uncertainty and ambiguity of contemporary attachments, individuals may resort to fundamentalism. We see evidence of this not only in America, but globally, as well, as both religious and ideological extremists create certainty through inflexible and exclusive belief systems. The other danger is drift. Individuals may become so relativistic in their outlooks that they are unable to come to terms with the validity of belief systems for themselves or for others, and thus may lose any powerful sense of meaning, belonging, or commitment. Sandel speaks of the need, as do others, for a self-reflexive understanding that permits us to be attached, with all the attendant benefits, and yet, to remain conscious of those attachments. We would be neither members of a well-integrated gemeinschaft, unaware of our own attachments, nor members of a weakly networked gesellschaft, whose only shared belief is the right to protect our own interests. He suggests instead a type of attachment that helps to locate us in particular communities while allowing us to see our interdependence with others, regionally, nationally, and internationally.[38]

Sociologist Daniel Bell[39] recently commented on this effort to balance attachment and transcendent freedom in his own life.

> [I am] Jewish in the fundamental sense that people always live in tension between particularity and universal notions. If you're entirely universal, you've become deracinated. You have no roots. If you're entirely particularized, you're rather narrowed by the orthodoxy of your creed and your belief. So, it seems to me my whole life has always been lived in that sense of the tension between the particular and the universal, at times, moving towards one or another pole.

Seyla Benhabib[40] has suggested that the work of Habermas provides a way to balance the benefits of civic republicanism, whose emphasis on the particular may be too confining in contemporary societies, and procedural liberalism, whose rational universalism fails to provide sufficient depth of attachment under modern conditions. For Habermas, this third way is the "discursive model of public space." Habermas[41] conceptualizes an interrelated social and political system composed of several parts: civil society, with organized and unorganized elements within it; a public sphere; an organized political system; and the constitutional state. Habermas's model is discussed in further detail in chapter 2; it is relied on to locate the realm of civil ethics that is proposed there. For our purposes here, it is useful to note what he says about civil society: "The core of civil society comprises a network of associations that institutionalizes problem-solving discourses on questions of general interest inside the framework of organized public spheres."[42]

The public sphere, for Habermas, is the realm that exists between civil society and the organized governmental sector. It is the arena in which discussions based on "the public use of reason"[43] emerge; this sphere further distills and refines the opinions emerging from civil society. The sphere is open and reflexive. Benhabib[44] comments on Habermas's view of the public sphere:

> Public space is not understood agonistically as a space of competition for acclaim and immortality among a political elite; it is viewed democratically as the creation of procedures whereby those affected by general social norms and collective political decisions can have a say in their formulation, stipulation, and adoption.

Above the public sphere is the organized political system, which in most complex industrial societies is a representative system of governance, based on the assumption of conflicting interests.[45] Here discourses reach the possibility of being transformed from "opinion formation" into "will formation" as debate, dialogue, and occasionally deliberation result in new laws. The laws are part of the constitutional state and, while providing the procedures for a democratic society, are themselves the result of "moral" discourse. Habermas reminds us that the constitutional framework itself originally grew out of and continues to evolve from intense discussion, public reasoning, and formal deliberation.[46]

Habermas and Rawls, as well as Alexis de Tocqueville,[47] have seen the associations of civil society as a training ground on which individuals begin the process of discourse and discussion; these discussions may clarify what kinds of short-term and long-term interests participants have in a policy matter. Participation by citizens in shared activities or in shared cultural events, such as reading books, listening to music, attending the theater, watching television, observing sports, and involvement in public forums of various types, may lead to recognition of common interests that may later be more fully articulated under formal deliberative procedures. This book is concerned with uncovering and discovering how discussion and participation in civil society about the future of the environment may become more formally linked to deliberations in the public sphere(s) and governmental sector(s), at the local, state, national, and international levels, such that the accepted principles emanating from these activities may provide a basis for developing a civil ethics about our future.

This book is thus an attempt to understand: (1) how viable the linkages are, or perhaps can be made to be, between community and the polity under modern conditions; (2) how the relationship between the largely private and strongly integrative ties of community and the more public, but restricted, attachments of the polity can serve the creation of a realm of civil ethics; and (3) how such an ethos can be usefully applied to decisions about the future well-being of the biosphere.

Rawls[48] indicates that the public discussion of justice, as we begin the twenty-first century, should probably include concerns about future generations, international law, health care, and animals and nature. All of these concerns, in one way or another, touch upon the future of humans' relationship with each other and with the millions of species with whom we share the biosphere. That, and how we can begin to uncover and discover whether we have any common interests on these matters, translate them into policy and program goals, and articulate them into a set of ethics to help guide our actions in the future, is the central focus of this book.

BACKGROUND: CONTEMPORARY ENVIRONMENTAL POLICY AND POLITICS IN THE UNITED STATES AND THE CONCEPT OF SUSTAINABLE DEVELOPMENT

Humans, of course, have varying concerns about the natural environment and the priority it should take among policy issues. Using a Hegelian dialectic, Allan Schnaiberg[49] suggests that ideologies about the conservation and protection of the environment may be conceptualized by looking at the interplay between two contending forces and sets of interests in modern societies: those forces and those interests that place the highest value on economic growth and put that goal ahead of all others in policy debates, and those forces and those interests that place the highest value on environmental protection and conservation and put that goal ahead of all others in policy debates.[50] The outcome of the confrontation between those defending economic growth as the dominant social value (thesis) and those defending environmental protection as the most important priority (antithesis) produces a new synthesis in society; the synthesis, however, is shaped by how successful the contending forces have been in institutionalizing their policy priorities. One outcome of this conflict may be that economic values will be triumphant. In the history of modern American environmental politics, this thesis dominated in the postwar years from 1945 to 1960. Following the end of World War II and the unleashing of vast industrialized economic forces, the nation focused on economic growth, as a new middle class moved to the suburbs, started families, and had more disposable income with which to fuel a consumer economy.[51] Schnaiberg[52] argues that a second synthesis began to emerge in the 1960s. He calls this second synthesis "managed scarcity," as the forces of economic growth came into full contention with the forces for environmental protection. The social movement that pushed for environmental protection in the 1960s had many antecedents. These included the evidence that unregulated industrial growth was resulting in visible air and water pollution; the emergence of critics of unbridled materialism in the 1950s and 1960s, such as Paul Goodman, Herbert Marcuse, and Murray Bookchin; the publication of *Silent Spring* by Rachel Carson in 1962; and the general reevaluation of major institutions in this society by students, civil rights activists, and women.[53] The clash between the forces favoring economic growth and those favoring environmental protection ushered in the era of managed scarcity. The U.S. Congress responded, between 1969 and 1979, by passing major pieces of legislation that became the institutionalized base of environmental protection in the United States; these laws include the Clean Air Act, the Clean Water Act, the Endangered Species Act, and the Resources Conservation and Recovery Act.[54]

By the late 1970s and the early 1980s, the forces and interests that favored economic growth once again had achieved dominance. The election of Ronald Reagan in 1980—and with that, the ascendance of the "sagebrush rebels"[55] and the appointment of cabinet secretaries and agency directors whose ideologies of unfettered economic growth often ran counter to the legislated missions of their departments and agencies—signaled an executive reorientation to unhindered economic growth. The government of the Reagan years should still be seen as operating under a "managed scarcity" synthesis, however. The backlash against Ronald Reagan's policies in the mid-1980s, and George H. W. Bush's choice to run under the mantle of "environmental president" in 1988, indicate that the forces for conservation and preservation were still a significant part of the national discussion about the future of the environment. Although the Clinton administration also focused primarily on economic growth, it did act to prevent any weakening, by the Gingrich Congress, of the environmental statutes passed in the 1970s, and it used its executive authority to further the acquisition of public lands in the West.[56] It is also well to remember that Al Gore, who clearly has associated himself with the importance of environmental protection and conservation, received more popular votes than George W. Bush in the 2000 election (although the analysis of what his popularity rested on is yet to be written), while the environmental policy proposals of President George W. Bush, reminiscent of those of the Reagan administration, have faced serious criticism, both nationally and internationally (see chapters 4 and 5).

Schnaiberg also proposed a third synthesis: an ecological one. Here the priority would be on environmental protection and conservation. He understood that probably no modern society has actually used this synthesis as its guiding orientation, although some of the Scandinavian nations and some countries of western Europe have come close, with serious attention to integrating environmental goals into economic development and planning. One notion that has emerged from policy discussions over these issues since the mid-1980s has been the concept of "sustainable development." As first used by the World Commission on Environment and Development in 1987 in their report *Our Common Future*,[57] sustainable development was defined as "development that meets the needs of the present without compromising the ability of future generations to meet their own needs." Sustainable development marks an important integration of the ideology supportive of economic growth and the ideology supportive of environmental protection.

Sustainable development focuses on two types of inequalities that threaten the future of the environment. One is intergenerational. Here the concern is with those presently on the planet using resources at such a rate or producing long-lasting pollutants at such a rate that the earth's ecosystems will not be able to adjust to the imbalanced chemical cycles and energy flows, threatening the ability of future generations to have a desirable quality of life. The second type of inequality is an intragenerational one; this concerns the vast discrepancy of wealth and life prospects between the 20 percent of the planet's inhabitants living in the developed nations and the 80 percent of the planet's inhabitants living in the developing nations.[58] The World Commission and others have argued that the developing nations will need to increase their economic growth so that their quality of life, infant mortality rates, life expectancy rates, and income per capita approach those of the developed nations. Such economic growth could be premised on sound environmental principles that incorporate incentives for developing new patterns of production and consumption that utilize new technologies that are less material and energy intensive. The World Commission suggested that it is the responsibility of the developed nations, whose economic growth has been based, until recently, on being able to freely use natural sinks to dispose of industrial wastes, to now help the less developed nations of the world, either through the transfer of more expensive, but environmentally safer, technologies or through funds that will help those nations develop innovative technologies on their own. While the developed nations would be asked to more efficiently use resources and more effectively control pollution, and to place some limits on their economic growth, the developing nations would be allowed (environmental) room to achieve economic growth.[59] It was in fact the articulation of separate goals for lowering greenhouse gases for the developed and developing nations that prompted the Republican-controlled Congress in the 1990s and the George W. Bush administration in 2001 to reject the Kyoto Treaty, which almost all the other developed nations of the world have now accepted.[60]

For some who favor economic development as a primary value, the concept of sustainable development goes too far in placing environmental limits on economic growth. For some whose primary value is environmental protection, sustainable development allows too much economic growth and allows the proponents of economic growth to cloak their goals for growth in an environmental mantle. The usefulness of sustainable development as a mechanism to guide both growth and environmental protection in the following decades will depend on the actual agreements worked out in its name. Yet what the concept of sustainable development has helped to provide, in the closing decades of the twentieth century, is the understanding that limits may have to be set on how humans use resources and produce pollution and that we have responsibilities to those humans with whom we currently share the planet, to future generations, and to other species. How then to link discussion of and participation in key environmental issues in the United States to deliberative mechanisms in the public and governmental spheres, and how emergent shared understandings from these activities may eventually be translated into a set of civil ethics that can help guide the development of more environmentally sustainable local, state, national, and international goals and policies, are the subjects explored in the remainder of this book.

NOTES

1. See Michael Sandel, *Democracy's Discontent: America in Search of a Public Philosophy* (Cambridge, Mass.: Belknap Press of Harvard University Press, 1996); Robert Bellah, *The Broken Covenant: American Civil Religion in Time of Trial* (Chicago: University of Chicago Press, 1992); Martin E. Marty, *The One and the Many: America's Struggle for the Common Good* (Cambridge, Mass.: Harvard University Press, 1997); Robert D. Putnam, *Bowling Alone: The Collapse and Revival of American Community* (New York: Simon & Schuster, 2001); and Robert Wuthnow, *Loose Connections: Joining Together in America's Fragmented Communities* (Cambridge, Mass.: Harvard University Press, 1998).

2. G. Tyler Miller Jr., *Living in the Environment: Principles, Connections, and Solutions*, 12th ed. (Belmont, Calif.: Wadsworth/Thomson Learning, 2002), 2–41.

3. Herschel Elliott and Richard Lamm, "A Moral Code for a Finite World," *The Chronicle Review*, 15 November 2002, 7–9 (B).

4. See Lin Yutang, ed., *The Wisdom of China and India* (New York: Random House, 1942), 811–813.

5. See Roger Fisher and William Ury, *Getting to Yes: Negotiating Agreement without Giving In*, ed. Bruce Patton, 2nd ed. (New York: Penguin, 1991); and Jane Mansbridge, *Beyond Adversary Democracy* (Chicago: University of Chicago Press, 1983), 252–269.

6. See Amy Gutmann and Dennis Thompson, *Democracy and Disagreement* (Cambridge, Mass.: Belknap Press of Harvard University Press, 1996), 1–9.

7. Michael E. Kraft and Norman J. Vig, "Environmental Policy from the 1970s to the Twenty-First Century," in *Environmental Policy: New Directions for the Twenty-First Century*, ed. Norman J. Vig and Michael E. Kraft (Washington, D.C.: Congressional Quarterly, 2003), 1–32.

8. See Ben A. Minteer and Bob Pepperman Taylor, eds., *Democracy and the Claims of Nature: Critical Perspectives for a New Century* (Lanham, Md.: Rowman & Littlefield, 2002), 1–10.

9. See Jürgen Habermas, *Between Facts and Norms: Contributions to a Discourse Theory of Law and Democracy*, trans. William Rehg (Cambridge, Mass.: MIT Press, 1996). The concepts of public sphere(s) and governmental sector(s) are explored more fully in chapter 2.

10. Ferdinand Tonnies, *Community and Society*, ed. Charles Loomis (1887; reprint, New York: Harper & Row, 1963).

11. Emile Durkheim, *The Elementary Forms of the Religious Life* (1911; reprint, New York: Free Press, 1965); Dennis Wrong, *The Problem of Order: What Unites and What Divides Society* (Cambridge, Mass.: Harvard University Press, 1994); Amitai Etzioni, *The Monochrome Society* (Princeton, N.J.: Princeton University Press, 2001).

12. Seyla Benhabib, "Models of Public Space: Hannah Arendt, the Liberal Tradition, and Jürgen Habermas," in *Habermas and the Public Sphere*, ed. Craig Calhoun (Cambridge, Mass.: MIT Press, 1996), 73–98.

13. Robert A. Dahl, *On Democracy* (New Haven, Conn.: Yale University Press, 1998), 7–25; Mansbridge, *Beyond Adversary Democracy*, 3–22.

14. James Bohman and William Rehg, eds., *Deliberative Democracy: Essays on Reason and Politics* (Cambridge, Mass.: MIT Press, 1999), ix–xxx.

15. Benhabib, "Models of Public Space," 73–98.

16. Sandel, *Democracy's Discontent*, 3–24, 123–249.

17. Bellah, *Broken Covenant*, 17–18.

18. Sandel, *Democracy's Discontent*, 250–274, 25–54; John Rawls, "The Idea of Public Reason: Postscript," in *Deliberative Democracy: Essays on Reason and Politics*, ed. James Bohman and William Rehg (Cambridge, Mass.: MIT Press, 1999), 93–144.

19. Sandel, *Democracy's Discontent*, 3–24.

20. Marty, *The One and the Many*, 203–204; Bellah, *Broken Covenant*, 172–173.

21. The second paragraph of the Declaration of Independence begins, "We

hold these truths to be self-evident, that all men are created equal; that they are endowed by their Creator with certain inalienable rights; that among these are life, liberty, and the pursuit of happiness." The preamble to the Constitution begins, "We the People of the United States, in Order to form a more perfect Union, establish Justice, insure Domestic Tranquility, provide for the common defence, promote the general Welfare, and secure the Blessings of Liberty to ourselves and our Posterity." Thomas E. Patterson, *We the People*, 4th ed. (Boston: McGraw-Hill, 2002), A, A5.

22. Sandel, *Democracy's Discontent*, 28.

23. Bellah, *Broken Covenant*, 1–35, 172–173.

24. Bellah, *Broken Covenant*, 53.

25. Sandel, *Democracy's Discontent*, 250–273.

26. John Rawls, *Justice as Fairness: A Restatement*, ed. Erin Kelly (Cambridge, Mass.: Belknap Press of Harvard University Press, 2001), 3.

27. Craig Calhoun, ed., *Habermas and the Public Sphere* (Cambridge, Mass.: MIT Press, 1996).

28. Rawls, *Justice as Fairness*, 3.

29. Calhoun, *Habermas and the Public Sphere*.

30. Rawls, *Justice as Fairness*, 5, 9.

31. Rawls, "The Idea of Public Reason," 93–130.

32. Sandel, *Democracy's Discontent*, 3–7, 91–122; Etzioni, *Monochrome Society*.

33. Putnam, *Bowling Alone*.

34. Wuthnow, *Loose Connections*.

35. Steven Brint, "Gemeinschaft Revisited: A Critique and Reconstruction of the Community Concept," *Sociological Theory* 19, no. 1 (March 2001): 1–23.

36. The Dalai Lama, *Ethics for a New Millennium* (New York: Riverhead Books, 1999).

37. Sandel, *Democracy's Discontent*, 317–352.

38. On the issue of "self-reflexiveness," see also Seyla Benhabib, *The Reluctant Modernism of Hannah Arendt* (Thousand Oaks, Calif.: Sage, 1996), 193–215, and Benhabib, "Models of Public Space."

39. Joseph Dorman, *Arguing the World: The New York Intellectuals in Their Own Words* (New York: Free Press, 2000), 11–12.

40. Benhabib, "Models of Public Space."

41. Habermas, *Between Facts and Norms*.

42. Habermas, *Between Facts and Norms*, 367.

43. A phrase used by Immanuel Kant, quoted in the introduction to Bohman and Rehg, *Deliberative Democracy*, 3.

44. Benhabib, "Models of Public Space," 87.

45. Mansbridge, *Beyond Adversary Democracy*.

46. Habermas, *Between Facts and Norms*.

47. John Stone and Stephen Mennell, eds., *Alexis de Tocqueville on Democracy, Revolution, and Society* (Chicago: University of Chicago Press, 1980).

48. Rawls, "The Idea of Public Reason," 117.

49. Allan Schnaiberg, *The Environment: From Surplus to Scarcity* (New York: Oxford University Press, 1980), 425.

50. Miller (*Living in the Environment*, 740–758) also proposes a typology of environmental ideologies that distinguishes between those that put humans (anthropocentric) at the center of their worldviews and those that put ecosystems (ecocentric) at the center. This typology is utilized in greater detail in chapter 4.

51. Schnaiberg, *The Environment*; Allan Schnaiberg and Kenneth Alan Gould, *Environment and Society: The Enduring Conflict* (New York: St. Martin's, 1994); Robert Gottlieb, *Forcing the Spring: The Transformation of the American Environmental Movement* (Washington, D.C.: Island, 1983).

52. Schnaiberg, *The Environment*.

53. Gottlieb, *Forcing the Spring*, 81–116.

54. Gottlieb, *Forcing the Spring*, 117–161; Miller, *Living in the Environment*, 23–42.

55. Those supporters of Ronald Reagan, in and out of government, who sought to limit the federal role in land and resources management became known as the "sagebrush rebels," identified with the plant (and ideal of freedom) associated with the western plains in the United States. See Miller, *Living in the Environment*, 35, 589.

56. Kraft and Vig, "Environmental Policy."

57. The World Commission on Environment and Development, *Our Common Future* (New York: Oxford University Press, 1987), 43.

58. Miller, *Living in the Environment*, 3–41; The World Commission, *Our Common Future*, 1–23.

59. The World Commission, *Our Common Future*, 1–98; Miller, *Living in the Environment*, 2–22; Schnaiberg, *The Environment*, 64–69.

60. Andrew Revkin, "178 Nations Reach a Climate Accord: U.S. Only Looks On," *New York Times*, 24 July 2001, 1, 7 (A); Andrew Revkin, "Global Warming Impasse Is Broken," *New York Times*, 11 November 2001, 8 (A).

2

Discussion, Participation, Deliberation, and Modern Community: Connections with Public Spheres, Governmental Sectors, Civil Ethics, and Environmental Values

> I am not here as a public official, but as a citizen of a troubled world who finds hope in a growing consensus that the generally accepted goals of society are peace, freedom, human rights, environmental quality, the alleviation of suffering and the rule of law.
>
> —Jimmy Carter, "Nobel Lecture"

Hannah Arendt argues that with the transition from the all-encompassing polity, which characterized the Greek and Roman city-states, to the modern nation-state, "society" became distinct from "the state." The family, the economy, and civil associations were now attached to the privatized domains of "society," while governing institutions were linked to the attenuated, but public, realm of the "state." It is Jürgen Habermas, more than Arendt, who sees the potential of these segmented private arenas to provide new opportunities for "public reasoning." Seyla Benhabib states:

> whereas Arendt sees a decline of the public sphere under conditions of modernity, Habermas notes the emergence of new forms of publicity in the

17

Enlightenment, that is, the public of private individuals reasoning together about public matters. . . . For Habermas, the public sphere is not just, or even principally, an arena of action but an impersonal medium of communication, information, and opinion formation.[1]

Many contemporary analysts[2] have made the further distinction between the purely private realms of the family and economy, and civil society, which is conceived as the nonprofit, independent, third sector, situated between this private realm and the public sphere of government. Tocqueville was among the first to recognize the dynamism of civil society in the United States; he observed its energy, vitality, and bustle. The associations comprising civil society served several important purposes. Through direct participation in these organizations, individuals developed the skills and the "habits of the heart"[3] necessary for self-government. These associations also provided a counterweight to the "state," preventing it from becoming out of touch, unaccountable, or despotic. Finally, these associations forced individuals to consider things beyond their own self-interest, linking their futures with those of other community members. Tocqueville[4] wrote: "For in a community in which ties of family, of caste, of class, and craft fraternities no longer exist, people are far too much disposed to think exclusively of their own interests, to become self-seekers practicing a narrow individualism and caring nothing for the public good."

Concern with community and the linking of individual desires to something greater than the self were important in the founding of America. Bellah[5] discusses the realm of civil religion, in which certain values, derived from spiritual or religious doctrines, also become the sacred values of the nation. "By civil religion I refer to that religious dimension, found I think in the life of every people, through which it interprets its historical experience in the light of transcendent reality."

A civil religion could provide guidance for individual lives, families, communities, and the nation; its meaning harkens back also to sociologist Emile Durkheim's distinction between the realms of the "sacred" and the "profane."[6] Durkheim analyzed the more mundane and prosaic arenas within which humans spent a considerable amount of time acquiring and maintaining the resources necessary for survival in primitive societies. There were also the less frequent and the more extraordinary times, when these individuals gathered together in celebration, accompanied perhaps by music, song, or dance, and were transported beyond their ordinary reality, becoming aware of something transcendent. Durkheim believed these moments were experienced by the groups as sacred; the sacred was memorialized by the establishment of a totem. Durkheim, a founder of modern sociology, argued that the transcendent reality the group became aware of was the manifestation of the social. In Durkheim's analysis, this realm acquires a reality of its own; the whole becomes more than merely the sum of its parts. It is through the social that norms and values are established and practices created that guide the daily lives of individuals; it is this same duality of "facts" and "norms" that is of interest to Habermas.[7]

The realm of civil religion as Bellah conceives it is partly derived from religious beliefs, but also clearly based on republican notions of virtue. Among these virtues are love of the community and individual self-restraint. He states:

> In Montesquieu's analysis, a republic will stand only so long as its citizens love it. If it needs external coercion its principle is lost. And Montesquieu, echoing many a hero of the early Roman republic, tells us that only frugality and the absence of luxury can keep the public interest in the minds of the citizens and make possible the renunciation of self which is so difficult but without which no republic can long survive.[8]

Jane Mansbridge[9] reminds us of another set of characteristics that sustained the polity of the Greek city-state: friendship and respect. She says: "Aristotle tells us that the Greeks saw a kind of solidarity, which they called 'friendship,' as the necessary basis for the state. Further, they identified equality, consensus, face-to-face contact, and common interests as distinguishing features of that friendship."

We may think then of civil religion as the realm in which citizens can be lifted out of the "profane"; it may fulfill the function, especially in more contemporary societies, of providing a set of unifying values, much as the polity and civic republic did in earlier ones. Among the core values honored in the American context are liberty and freedom, along with a concern for fairness, justice, equality, and tolerance. Fraternity or fellowship or friendship—as well as compassion and generosity, though less prominent—are also prized. These values are present, according to Bellah, in the founding documents of the nation, in the oratory and sermons of its leaders, and in the songs and hymns that guided the nation from its earliest years.[10]

The ideals expressed in these cultural statements, although perhaps unfulfilled to any significant degree at the time they were written, are the ideas that drove the nation to become what it is still in the process of becoming. In 1776, the Declaration of Independence proclaimed a vision, which certainly then was not and even now is not fully realized in the United States: "We hold these truths to be self-evident, that all men are created equal; that they are endowed by their Creator with certain unalienable rights; that among these, are life, liberty, and the pursuit of happiness."[11] Here the call to liberty, freedom, and equality is inescapable.

Writing "four score and seven years" later, Abraham Lincoln reiterated, "our fathers brought forth on this continent, a new nation, conceived in Liberty, and dedicated to the proposition that all men are created equal."[12] Lincoln also acknowledged the covenant with God and the search for justice in his second inaugural address on March 4, 1865.

> Neither party expected for the war, the magnitude, or the duration, which it has already attained. Neither anticipated that the *cause* of the conflict might cease with, or even before, the conflict itself should cease. Each looked for an easier triumph, and a result less fundamental and astounding. Both read the same Bible, and pray to the same God; and each invokes His aid against the other. It may seem strange that any men should dare to ask a just God's assistance in wringing their bread from the sweat of other men's faces; but let us judge not that we be not judged. The prayers of both could not be answered; that of neither has been answered fully. The Almighty has His own purposes.[13]

And of course the last paragraph of the speech displays an unerring vision of compassion, justice, community, and peace.

> With malice towards none; with charity for all; with firmness in the right, as God gives us to see the right, let us strive on to finish the work we are in; to bind up the nation's wounds; to care for him who shall have borne the battle, and for his widow, and his orphan—to do all which may achieve and cherish a just and lasting peace, among ourselves, and with all nations.[14]

When Lincoln later asked Frederick Douglass what he thought of the second inaugural address, Douglass called it a "sacred effort."[15] The vision of shared values and a shared fate is also present in the songs that the nation embraced in its early years, and that are sung still today. The act of singing can affect a community in several ways. There is first of all the music itself, which for some is a conduit to discover the sacred. There is also the shared experience of the group singing and of those who might simply be listening, which, as Durkheim hypothesized, may make individuals aware of something greater than themselves. Finally, there are the words as they are pronounced in public. Some of the best-known songs, now part of American culture, illustrate an awareness of a destiny that we share with each other, in the presence of nature's bounty. The words call on us, as Abraham Lincoln did in his first inaugural address, on March 4, 1861, to "not break our bonds of affection. The mystic *chords* of memory, stretching from every battlefield and patriot grave, to every living heart and hearth-stone, all over this broad land, will yet swell the *chorus* of the

Union, when again touched, as surely they will be, by the better angels of our nature."[16]

Many songs sung by Americans over the centuries have the power to evoke a sense of common purpose. They appeal to several ideals, including the covenant tradition; the liberty, freedom, equality, and fellowship for which America serves as a symbolic beacon; and the striking beauty of the landscape. Four songs, two from the nineteenth century and two from the twentieth, well illustrate these themes. *America (My Country 'Tis of Thee)*, written by Samuel Francis Smith in 1832, eloquently names freedom and liberty as America's hallmarks, while praising both its covenant with a higher power and its attachment to the land. *America the Beautiful*, written by Katherine Lee Bates in 1893, touches on these same themes and more; both its words and the music are deeply moving. The song describes the beauty of America, as well as its covenant with a higher power. It also alludes to several key civic republican themes: the limits we need to place on our selves, our duty to obey the law, and the bonds we form with our fellow citizens, creating something more important than any individual alone could realize. *God Bless America* was written by Irving Berlin in 1918, but not recorded until 1938. Berlin, a Russian Jewish immigrant to America, also wrote *White Christmas* and *Easter Parade*. *God Bless America* became an anthem of sorts for Americans following the events of September 11, 2001. It was sung by the members of the U.S. Congress on the steps of the Capitol soon after the collapse of the Twin Towers; at the reopening of the New York Stock Exchange on September 17, 2001; at churches, mosques, and synagogues throughout the land; and at countless vigils and countless public gatherings across the nation. It too addresses the covenant tradition, the hope of freedom, the magnificence of America's scenery, and the connections we share with each other in our "home." *This Land Is Your Land*, written by Woody Guthrie in 1940, was not published until 1954. Guthrie first wrote *This Land Is Your Land* using the title *God Blessed America*, in response to what he considered to be the overly nationalistic strains of Irving Berlin's song. Guthrie's complete song contains lyrics addressing the plight of the outsider, the migrant, and the homeless unable to find a place in America. Yet, it also offers a vision of the bounty that belongs to all of us as we learn to base our nation's future on respect, fellowship, and equality.[17]

It thus may be useful here to explore the relationship among the public sphere(s), governmental sector(s), and a locus that might be referred to as the realm of "civil ethics," especially as applied to the United States.[18] Of particular interest would be the dynamic quality of the public sphere(s) and governmental sector(s) in their interactions with a set of "sacred" values within the realm of civil ethics. The idea of sacred values offers us the possibility that some values and some virtues may in fact become acceptable to a diverse and complex citizenry, may be used in public reasoning, and may provide a basis for "will formation."[19] "Sacred values" here refers to ethics or virtues that may be derived from religious, moral, philosophical, or civic traditions, but that do not require the theological or metaphysical underpinnings of those traditions to be accepted or even used in public discussion. The intense understanding of, commitment to, and practice of a particular religious, metaphysical, or moral tradition have largely been, and should largely remain, part of the private sphere in the United States, including the family and some of the institutions of civil society. In trying to reclaim some of the advantages of a civic republic, without forfeiting the increased individual freedom, greater equality, and improved respect for diversity of the procedural republic, is it possible, in twenty-first-century America, to draw on aspects of these values and traditions and make use of them in public reasoning? Is it possible that, through the give-and-take of communication within the public sphere, we begin to develop some consensus about some of these values, so that they become part of an expanded understanding of the accepted principles that we draw on to guide opinion formation[20] in the public sphere and will formation in the governmental sector? Rawls alludes to this prospect when he says:

> When engaged in public reasoning may we also include reasons of our comprehensive doctrines? I now believe, and hereby I revise section 8 in "The Idea of Public Reason," that such reasonable doctrines may be introduced in public reason at any time, provided that in due course public reasons, given by a reasonable political conception, are presented sufficient to support whatever the comprehensive doctrines are introduced to support.[21]

Rawls thus acknowledges that these comprehensive belief systems may influence our values, and thereby influence the types of policy approaches we favor. He argues, however—and this is consistent with procedural liberalism, which he generally supports—that ultimately our reasons in public must be made acceptable to others without having to reference a notion of the good[22] as defined in a particular "comprehensive doctrine." After deliberation, however, there may be a consensus to support a path or urge action in the governmental sector that inevitably, as Sandel[23] argues, connotes support for one set of values rather than another. In the liberal procedural model, however, that set of policy preferences can easily be replaced by a different set when a majority chooses an alternate path. There is, thus, no enduring conception of the commonweal in the proceduralism of the liberal republic; there are only the policy approaches that a majority of the citizens support at a given time.

What perhaps then could be added to this conversation is the hypothesized existence of a realm of civil ethics, a realm that contains formative values, values that imply a set of enduring commitments or responsibilities to others and a set of restraints or limits that would apply to individuals, communities, and even societies as a whole. Although the values that may be said to comprise the civil ethos can be derived from comprehensive belief systems, their incorporation into the realm of civic ethics would result from the democratic dynamics of discussion, participation, and deliberation within civil society, the public sphere(s), and governmental sector(s), as well as discourse related to the constitutional framework itself. What distinguishes these values from the policy preferences that emerge ordinarily from the public sphere and governmental sectors is that these values have acknowledged prescriptive implications for a society in its public life. At the same time, they are distinct from the comprehensive belief systems from which they may be derived. The Dalai Lama, an individual strongly committed to the practice of one religious tradition, Tibetan Buddhism, makes the distinction between religious commitments and what he terms spiritual commitments.

> I believe there is an important distinction to be made between religion and spirituality. Religion I take to be concerned with faith in the claims to salvation of one faith tradition or another, an aspect of which is acceptance of some form of metaphysical or supernatural reality, including perhaps an idea of heaven or *nirvana*. Connected with these are religious teachings or dogma, ritual, prayer, and so on. Spirituality I take to be concerned with those qualities of the human spirit—such as love and compassion, patience, tolerance, forgiveness, contentment, a sense of responsibility, a sense of harmony—which bring happiness to both self and others.[24]

In terms particularly relevant to the relationship of human beings to one another and to the natural environment, there are at least four issues that might require formative responses because of their connection to what the distinguished biologist Edward O. Wilson[25] has characterized as "the future of life." Obviously, it will be through democratic deliberation that the full range of issues and values to be considered in these matters will emerge. The issues that perhaps should be central are the responsibilities a society and its members have toward: (1) the health and well-being of other humans with whom they presently share the planet; (2) the health and well-being of future generations that will eventually occupy the planet; (3) the health and well-being of the other species and the ecosystems with whom they share the planet, both now and in the future; and (4) cooperatively working on these matters with the other people and the other nations with whom they share the planet.

To see how these issues might be addressed with values derived from the realm of civil ethics, it might be helpful to discuss an institutional model of society that provides a location for that realm. The model, which makes use of some ideas developed by Habermas[26] and Rawls,[27] consists of (1) a private sphere, (2) the arena of civil society, (3) the public sphere(s), (4) the governmental sector(s), (5) the constitutional state, and (6) the realm of civil ethics. The private sphere would include the family and the economy, providing the base upon which civil society is built. Some analysts might argue against the placement of the economy in the private sphere in this model, both because institutionally it is increasingly integrated with the governmental sector, and because in terms of the earlier model of civic republicanism that existed in the United States, and to which this book is attempting to pay some homage, the central values of a society should suffuse individual experiences in all key institutions, including the economy. John Dewey, early in the twentieth century, argued that in encouraging the emergence of values and practices to create a truly democratic society, the private, industrial sector would also have to be transformed. Robert Westbrook quotes from Dewey's "The Ethics of Democracy": "all industrial relations are to be regarded as subordinate to human relations, to the law of personality. . . . They are to become the material of an ethical realization; the form and substance of a community of good (though not necessarily of goods) wider than any now known."[28]

For the purposes of this discussion, we can set aside the question of the transformation of industrial relations, not simply because it would require a radical alteration of the values and institutions of our present market-dominated economy, but also because industrial relations may be most democratically reformed if such changes were to emerge from the type of deliberations in the public sphere and governmental sectors that are being proposed here. Thus, the argument here will focus primarily on the relationships between individuals in communities and the organizations and institutions of civil society, the public sphere(s), the governmental sector(s), the constitutional framework, and the realm of the civil ethics. However, there is nothing here that would preclude these discussions, activities, and deliberations from also being pursued in the workplace. The three process variables that will provide the linkages between individuals in all of these realms are discussion, participation, and deliberation.[29]

Civil society is thus here conceived as that arena between the private sphere and the governmental sector. Habermas[30] suggests that civil society has both organized and unorganized elements to it. Civil society includes individuals as they exist in neighborhood/residential settings and participate in the plethora of neighborhood, community, and voluntary organizations; the variety of religious congregations; and the other variants of community engagement that modern analysts have suggested.[31] Spontaneous interactions by individuals within or between any of these organizations or institutions would constitute the unorganized component of civil society. Neighbors talking over the backyard fence, customers chatting at a local grocery or coffee shop, consumers exchanging pleasantries at the local mall may all be examples of this. Key to all of these relationships is what Putnam[32] and others have called "social capital": the "connections among individuals—social networks and the norms of reciprocity and trustworthiness that arise from them." Clearly, the density or looseness of these attachments is important, particularly in terms of the mutual expectations they generate.

Modern communal ties may be distinguishable from communal attachments of the past in the degree to which individuals are now freer to balance their commitments to others with their own needs for autonomy. This more voluntary nature of modern association also explains its reflexiveness; while socially engaged, individuals are now more aware of the engagement. This places greater responsibilities on individuals for social integration and invites the twin dangers of drift (when ties are extremely loose) and fundamentalism (when ties are extremely rigid), as Sandel[33] has noted. It also, however, offers new opportunities for individuals to choose their most significant bases of identity and communal involvement, the consolidation of which may provide a locus for greater individual satisfaction and fulfillment. Though potentially complicating social relations, this understanding about our own selves may provide a basis for recognizing the "natality" and "mortality" of others, something that analysts such as Arendt consider central to comprehending "the human condition."[34]

Above the organizations and the institutions of civil society is the public sphere, located between civil society and the governmental sector. Rawls[35] suggests that we conceive of the public sphere as existing at several levels, including the local, national, and international planes. It is within the public sphere that the process of "opinion formation" occurs,[36] and, as indicated earlier, it is largely a place of communication and information exchange.[37] The public sphere in contemporary societies is varied and complex. It includes a vast, integrated, and globalized network of communication: television, radio, newspapers, the Internet, books, films, music, theater, and sports. It can be at once impersonal, and yet quite meaningful, to the individuals who participate in shared content, activities, or communication connected to these phenomena. Habermas[38] reminds us that the public sphere is very dynamic; opinions formed run into their counterparts, leaving them perhaps unchanged, maybe modified, or possibly radically transformed. The discussions of the public sphere can originate in the private realm of the family or workplace, can move through the organs of civil society, and then may be taken up through the discursive transmission of modern communications into the public sphere—or can travel via any combination of these conduits into the public sphere. The public sphere should also be conceived of as including public forums, whether conducted in town squares; on the premises of municipal, state, or federal governments or university campuses; or through interactive television or Internet conferences. This represents a level of discussion, participation, and deliberation distinct from the formal institutions of the government sector. In fact, one argument of this book is that we need to create more places in the public sphere for meaningful deliberation whose policy recommendations can be transferred to the official and accountable institutions of government for further discussion, deliberation, and implementation.

The governmental sector consists of all of the institutions and personnel of the res publica[39] with their legislative, executive, administrative, and judicial functions, at the local, state, national, and international levels. It is within the governmental sector that "will formation" takes place.[40] The discussions, activities, and deliberations that have taken place in the public sphere and within the institutions of the governmental sector may here be formalized into policies and programs. In most contemporary democracies, the legislative branch of government is a representative institution that operates under the assumptions of what Mansbridge[41] has called "adversary democracy." Although there may be face-to-face discussions, either in committees or on the floor of a chamber, there is no assumption that the participants in those discussions have common interests or that consensus is likely or even desirable. Here majority rules, when at least half of the discussants are willing to agree on a course of action. Referendums and initiatives, which do allow for direct citizen participation in policy decisions, are adversarial processes, as well.[42]

In the United States, the blueprint for the structure and processes of our governing system is, of course, the Constitution. Habermas[43] observes that even the founding documents of a nation illustrate a "discourse model of society"; the early debates about the nature and role of government in the United States, for instance, were intense face-to-face discussions about, among other things, how localized or centralized governmental power should be and how direct participation in governmental decision making should be. And the continuing discussions—among the public, elected officials, and members of the judiciary—over what the Constitution means provide evidence that the discourse is ongoing. The reigning public philosophy of the late twentieth century has eschewed a focus on values.[44] When values have entered public discussions, they have tended to be based on a narrow, rigid, and conservative religious theology. Controversial issues, such as abortion or gay rights, are framed in either the language of neutrality and the right to privacy derived from procedural liberalism or the language of sin and abomination derived from a cramped contemporary civic republican perspective. There has been little room in contemporary public or constitutional discourse for an affirmative view of individual freedom within a context of shared communal responsibilities.[45]

Finally, the hypothesized realm of civil ethics may be said to surround, to infuse, and, in turn, to be shaped by the public sphere(s), the governmental sector(s), and constitutional discourse(s),[46] as well as by the relationships, organizations, and institutions of civil society. The linkages between these arenas may be conceived of as discussion, participation, and deliberation. Discussion is here envisioned as simple conversation; in the American context, it often has one of two characteristics. On the one hand, it may be very vague or superficial, which some analysts have credited for the tolerance and equanimity of American culture. As John A. Hall and Charles Lindholm note:

an easygoing, friendly demeanor allows strangers to negotiate a social minefield where there are no clear status markers and where authority is decentralized and relatively weak; this unstable and potentially threatening universe is made livable by the expectation that one's friendliness and helpfulness will be returned.[47]

On the other hand, as Mansbridge notes, in a polity as large and diverse as ours, the assumption must be that our interests on policy matters will likely be in conflict.

the larger the polity, the more likely that individuals will have conflicting interests. . . . [T]he more individual interests come in conflict, the more a democracy encompassing those interests must employ adversary procedures. These two premises demand the conclusion that democracies as large as the modern nation-state be primarily adversary democracies.[48]

Perhaps it is the sense that our ultimate interests may be in conflict that moves us away from discussing controversial subjects in our daily encounters. In addition, the two-party political system in the United States tends to focus political preferences on the moderate, if muddled, center of the political spectrum. The use of a secret ballot in voting also allows us to avoid confronting our political differences.[49] Yet, when we move beyond vague generalities, public discussion of issues—particularly as conducted on contemporary talk shows—veers toward the other extreme. These shows seem to revel in and promote a polarizing approach to political discussion; participants gleefully seek to undermine any semblance of validity in the opposing speakers' comments, and rarely, if ever, discover any common ground. And yet, of course, simple discussions in civil society, the public sphere, and the governmental sector, or debates about the Constitution, have the potential to lead to greater understanding about the unique experiences of others and the shared nature of human tribulations.

Participation in activities at any of these levels also provides what Robert K. Merton[50] labels the "latent function of social life." While the manifest function of participation may be to complete a set of tasks or projects, these activities also build social ties among individuals whose backgrounds and experiences may be quite different. From the act of doing with others, whether participating in a neighborhood garage sale or community chorus, working on a local food drive or home rehabilitation, volunteering for a youth program or senior center, joining a book club or bowling league, a sense of camaraderie may emerge among people who heretofore knew little about each other. America, more than other countries, has always provided vast opportunities for people to participate in this way. Although analysts are not in agreement over whether the rates of participation in civil society have declined in recent years[51] or have merely changed in form,[52] there is little doubt that such participation is still a vital part of American culture and the American experience. To what extent such participation builds reservoirs of trust between human beings, in particular settings or the society at large, is the subject of contemporary social research. To what extent such participation also allows for the sharing of ideas beyond the more genial and superficial transactions of normal everyday life is a potentially significant research question. And the extent to which such participation resonates with, reflects, or infuses the principles that may be said to characterize the realm of civil ethics in society would require more systematic study to help us uncover. Certainly, it would be reasonable to at least hypothesize that such shared activities may allow individuals to get beyond their more mundane emotions, biases, and preconceptions to glimpse something beyond themselves, something that may suggest to them the common good.

Deliberation, on the other hand, is a conscious attempt to move beyond the simply apparent to that which may lie beneath (or above, depending perhaps on your philosophical perspective). It is a more formal and structured pattern of communication, whose purpose is to help uncover common threads and shared concerns. Analysts such as Arendt and Habermas[53] especially emphasize the *transformative* quality of deliberation: a conception, an understanding, a resolution of an issue may emerge from disparate elements whose connections may not have been obvious before. Joshua Cohen also observes:

> Deliberation, then, focuses debate on the common good. And the relevant conceptions of the common good are not comprised simply of interests and

preferences that are antecedent to deliberation. Instead, the interests, aims, ideals that comprise the common good are those that survive deliberation, interests that, on public reflection, we think it legitimate to appeal to in making claims on social resources.[54]

For Arendt and Habermas, the process of deliberation is its own justification; the potential to reach new insights, to move beyond self-interest, to unearth what may be the commonweal, provides the rationale for deliberation. More pragmatic analysts, such as Rawls and Cohen, while recognizing the evolution of preferences that may occur during deliberation, nonetheless believe that deliberative processes should be judged by how well they promote fairness and justice.[55]

Effective deliberation has a number of prerequisites, including access to relevant information and expertise, a rough equality of power and skills, and/or a measure of respect and trust among the participants.[56] Our jury system is premised on the random selection of individuals who, in approximating the local citizenry, stand for them when making a decision about the fate of a fellow citizen, using face-to-face deliberation. These ordinary citizens are confronted with the tremendous responsibility of moving beyond their personal preferences, biases, and emotional attachments in order to comprehend the facts and arguments of a case and arrive at the "correct solution":[57] a unanimous decision about the guilt or innocence of the defendant, at least in criminal cases. If they cannot reach a decision, if they become a hung jury, they have failed to find an answer to that question.

In the brilliant movie *Twelve Angry Men*, written by Reginald Rose in 1954,[58] the dramatic tension revolves around the jurors' original reluctance to move beyond their initial or superficial or biased impressions of the facts of the case. Some of the jurors are portrayed as simply apathetic or impatient, not caring very much about the case, eager to get on with their own lives, annoyed at the inconvenience of jury service. Other jurors are notably more charged with emotion, quick to pronounce the defendant guilty, but apparently suffering under the sway of their own demons. What Rose refers to as "anger" in the title may in fact be many different emotions or states of mind; except in the case of one juror, however, these feelings prevent the jurors from possessing the equanimity to carefully examine the relevant facts and arguments and arrive at a fair verdict. It is thus not intellectual incompetence, but emotional, ethical, or even spiritual lapses, that at first thwart the jurors in rendering a just outcome in this case. It is only the determination of the one juror, willing to bear the resentment of his peers, that sparks a real *re-view* of the evidence and the beginnings of a true deliberation. As each juror is freed from the emotions that have kept him from fairly evaluating the case, he is able to bring new insights to the puzzle of the defendant's guilt or innocence. The movie illustrates two important aspects of deliberative processes. First, there must be some mechanism, some pathway, that facilitates the participants' moving beyond initial impressions, initial biases, initial resistances, to see the issue or question at hand from less clouded vantage points. This may be promoted by structurally designed mechanisms or other processes that help the participants to understand they have a common interest in honestly addressing the questions before them. Second, the import of deliberation arises from the synthesis of the separate perspectives that each of the participants potentially can provide, producing a resolution that none may have otherwise foreseen.

Mansbridge[59] notes that, in unitary systems, which are based on the assumption of common interests, conflict is not eliminated. Instead, in a true deliberation, the parties continue to talk until they arrive at the answer on which all can agree. If no answer is agreeable to all, in systems that require unanimity, no decision is made. Other systems allow the majority to decide after sufficient deliberation has taken place. There is, of course, the danger of false consensus when decisions are made face-to-face. Particularly in a society, like ours, whose members shy away from expressing political opinions—at least in public settings—it may take a great deal of deliberative experience (and other conditions, including protection from retribution) before citizens feel comfortable in voicing objections to conclusions with which they do not agree. While face-to-face discussions may make individuals reluctant to state a contrary opinion, these settings provide opportunities to clear up misconceptions and misunderstandings. They can, in fact, lead to feelings of increased respect among the participants. Mansbridge notes that the Quakers, who make all their decisions by consensus, do this in fact because "consensus encourages the members to listen carefully to one another and to respect the others' experience or point of view."[60]

The advantage in trying to reach a decision by consensus, if it is done freely and without any of the participants feeling coerced, is that the decision reflects the concerns and preferences of all of those present. Presumably, 100 percent of the participants are comfortable with the outcome. In contrast, when majority rule is used—especially in conjunction with a secret ballot, as in adversary systems—a decision may satisfy only slightly more than half the participants. Mansbridge[61] argues that groups should learn to move between unitary and adversary procedures, depending on whether the participants feel they have been or may be able to uncover a common interest in the matter before them. If they have a common interest, they should use unitary procedures; if they can't discover a common interest, they should use adversary procedures. Adversary procedures better protect individual interests in policy matters; unitary procedures, however, may produce better decisions. Mansbridge notes that adversarial procedures can be made more sensitive to participants' preferences by the employment of mechanisms other than simple majority rule, such as proportional outcomes. Mansbridge also points out that, in unitary systems, the power and skills of the participants do not have to be equal, a fact with which most Americans, who are accustomed to using adversary procedures, may not be initially comfortable.[62] If the group or organization is pursuing what it believes to be a common interest, the only thing that needs to be equal is the participants' respect for each other. In adversary situations, on the other hand, safeguards must be employed to ensure that all the participants' interests are protected equally in the decision-making process. It is here that most attention may need to be paid to providing mechanisms that help to balance the power and skills of the participants.[63]

What may be crucial in making deliberation a significant part of democratic decision making is linking it to formal political institutions. Deliberation in this way may become a conduit for the "subjectless communication" of the public sphere;[64] it may also link citizens to their elected representatives in a potentially meaningful way. At least two variants of deliberation have been proposed in recent years. In one, citizens are selected randomly for their participation in a deliberative process, but are given access to the information and expertise they will need to make a decision. In the second, specific interests to the deliberation are separately represented in the deliberative process. Robert Dahl and James S. Fishkin provide good examples of the first, while Nancy E. Abrams and Joel R. Primack provide a model for the second.[65]

Several years ago, political theorist Robert Dahl[66] lamented the state of modern democracy in America; although an earlier proponent of pluralism and the role of interest groups in maintaining a vital, balanced, and accountable democracy, Dahl had become perturbed by trends in American life that threatened to undermine the role of interest groups in governance. One trend involved the increased influence of money in political campaigns, particularly with the formation of political action committees in the early 1970s, which diminished the power of ideas as the sole or most important determinant of a group's impact on policy outcomes.[67] This problem was then compounded by the increasingly complex and technical nature of emerging policy issues, from nuclear weapons to global warming, which threatened to limit the ability of average citizens to meaningfully participate in policy discussions. Dahl thus writes of the increased reliance on experts, both within and outside of government, and the decreased role of ordinary citizens in public deliberations as a threat to democracy; the most profound and important questions of the polity would now be "delegated" to those believed to be most informed on these subjects. He notes:

> Then we have not simply *delegated* authority. Instead, we have alienated con-
> trol over our lives to others: that is, for practical purposes we simply lose
> control over crucial decisions, and lose control over our lives. The more we
> alienate authority, rather than delegate it on terms that allow us to retain a
> meaningful degree of final control, the more we lose our freedom, and the
> more hollow the democratic process becomes.[68]

One suggestion Dahl has to "retain a meaningful degree of final control" over such decisions is the creation of a mechanism he called a "mini-populus." The minipopulus is a nod to the Greek ideal, premised on the notion that all citizens are fit to serve. In this model, however, randomly selected citizens are also given access to the information they will need to make informed decisions. Up to one thousand citizens, chosen at random, would be asked to deliberate on a particular policy issue for up to a year. Members of the minipopulus would have the resources to hear from a variety of experts, interest groups, concerned citizens, industry represen-tatives, government officials, and any others having something relevant to add to the discussion. After gathering the information they needed, the members of the minipopulus would deliberate and produce a set of recommendations; these recommendations would then be submitted to a legislative body or elected executive for final approval and implementa-tion. In making these recommendations, the minipopulus would "stand for"[69] the entire citizenry of the state or region or nation from which they had been selected. They would be representative of this population except in one respect: after one year of study, they would know more than the average citizen on the given subject. Their recommendations would be transferred to elected officials, however, since only elected officials would be directly accountable to the populace. Clearly, a model like this could work only if citizens had the time, desire, and supports that would be needed to participate in such a process. Only a society that valued citizen participation, public deliberation, and a search for the commonweal on important, but potentially divisive, issues would seek to implement such mechanisms in the first place. A society that valued civic engagement, and not just production and consumption activities, might also be the kind of society that would take more seriously the longer-term environ-mental consequences of its decisions, rather than just the short-term eco-nomic efficiencies. This same society might therefore exhibit more concern for the future well-being of the planet and its inhabitants.

Fishkin[70] also relies on a random sample of citizens in his deliberative polling process. Here, individuals are selected to receive a survey on a particular policy matter. Later, a smaller, but representative, group of the survey recipients is asked to deliberate face-to-face on the same matter. Fishkin later repolls these participants to see whether their ideas and attitudes have changed after face-to-face discussions. Fishkin's model could perhaps be modified, particularly for more technically challenging matters, so that the participants who met face-to-face would also be given access to information needed to help guide their deliberations. If Fishkin or others were still interested in measuring the impacts of face-to-face deliberation on decisions, as well as the role of information in that process, an experiment could be designed in which some groups would be given access to information, while others would not, and the types of information given to the groups would vary.

In the model proposed by Abrams and Primack,[71] different interests in a policy dispute are separately represented in the deliberations in a procedure called "critical review and public assessment." Abrams and Primack discuss this procedure in relation to the issue of nuclear waste disposal in Sweden. The process began with the government asking the nuclear utility to design a plan for waste disposal, based on the assumption that the industry itself would be intimately familiar with the complex issues involved in disposal. The industry proposal was then reviewed by a panel of experts commissioned by the government, highlighting the need for a first line of highly trained individuals to interpret and review such a proposal. The presence of a variety of experts at this stage also recognizes the fact that experts themselves may not agree. Even at this stage in the process, the experts, who by professional training and standards should be "objective" about the policy issues under review, are still not "value-free." Their philosophical, religious, or spiritual commitments may affect how they interpret even the same set of empirical findings. For instance, in the case of nuclear waste disposal, those more concerned about the dangers of nuclear power might evaluate the proposal differently than those less concerned about the dangers of nuclear power. Those who are employed by or have been consultants to the nuclear industry might evaluate the proposal differently than those who have been critics of the industry. "Dissenting" experts can interpret the same empirical findings differently because there are no safety limits carved in stone. Judgments need to be made about the set of facts, particularly in cases of environmental contamination; the guidelines are often based on laboratory experiments, which have their own set of limitations. These include the problem of an accurate dose-response curve, the need to extrapolate findings on animals to human subjects, and the often unknown set of exposures or synergistic effects of toxic compounds under real circumstances.[72] The "critical review" phase of this process acknowledges the diversity of judgments in such technical analysis, not only by commissioning, in this case, fifty reviews, but also by using a process that Abrams and Primack call "scientific mediation"; it is designed to "bring out the real trade-offs, both qualitative and quantitative, in such a technical plan."[73]

Once the experts have a chance to digest, interpret, discuss, and debate the industry's recommendations, their findings are made available for general public discussion. The "public assessment" phase of the process could commence with a meeting of groups representing a variety of interests or perspectives on the issue, including those chosen because of geographic, professional and work, or ideological affiliations, among others; they would convene to discuss the experts' findings. This public forum would produce a set of recommendations to be examined and further discussed by elected legislators or the chief executive. Abrams and Primack's approach supports a Habermasian discourse model of society: separate discussions and analyses feed back into each other and help to amend and improve the plan before the legislators or the chief executive makes the final decision. The plan also manages to include some of the major competing interests in many contemporary environmental disputes: industry; experts, in the diversity of their opinions; the public, represented in a variety of ways; and the government.

All of these models raise at least four issues that must be addressed for deliberative processes to be effective. There is first the matter of having sufficient information to arrive at what Mansbridge calls an "enlightened preference."[74] This is the policy position people would choose "if their information were perfect, including the knowledge they would have in retrospect if they had a chance to live out the consequences of each choice before actually making a decision." This echoes Dahl's notion that at least one of the obstacles to citizens successfully participating in modern policy decisions is their lack of knowledge or information about a given complex subject. However, Dahl and others are not arguing that citizens themselves must become experts; instead, these theorists believe that citizens have to be informed enough to be able to interpret and judge the validity of experts' advice. In Dahl's model, citizens are given access to the vast array of expertise; in Abrams and Primack's model, dissenting experts are given the job of initial interpretation. While both these models recognize a clear role for experts in decision making, they also underscore that the decision should not end with the experts.

This leads to a second facet of deliberation: beyond the technical risk issues that may have to be weighed in a policy matter, and whose elucidation by experts may be crucial, there are other factors that may also need to be included in a policy assessment. These may involve the economic, social, cultural, psychological, and other impacts of the policy under consideration; these factors too may call for expert input. However, in the end, political, philosophical, moral, ethical, spiritual, and religious beliefs and commitments may affect the weight that one assigns to any of these factors, even with the best information available. Thus, a deliberative process may also have to encourage its participants to make explicit their value commitments before they can begin to define for themselves what they believe to be the common interest or public good in the matter before them. As Rawls[75] notes, we may have to refer to our comprehensive doctrines in public deliberations, but ultimately, in dealing with the public good (as opposed to the good of what may be a nonpublic organization in civil society), we must find a means to justify our reasons to others in a way that does not rely on comprehensive doctrines to which they may not subscribe.

Third, a deliberative process also may need to provide a mechanism to address the prejudices, biases, or resistances that individuals may have that prevent them from viewing the matters before them without great distortion: these may have to be explicitly acknowledged before deliberation can effectively proceed. Thus, while the issues surrounding individuals' comprehensive doctrines *may* be viewed as "positive" attachments, the issues or states of mind that can distort perceptions and undermine the chance to define a common interest in a policy matter may be viewed as "negative" attachments. As Roger Fisher and William Ury[76] observe about establishing a hospitable environment for deliberations, "Freed from the burden of unexpressed emotions, people will become more likely to work on the problem." And finally, there is the issue of trust. If in fact the participants feel that they can trust the others involved in the deliberation, then the basis for generating respect is more secure. If, on the other hand, the participants do not trust one another, and the power or skill differentials among them are so great that they fear retribution and/or manipulation, then a deliberation cannot proceed along an authentic course.

Thus the subject of the deliberation, the method by which the participants to the deliberation are chosen, the degree to which the participants come to the deliberation with conflicts based on either negative attachments or positive commitments—or both—and the degree to which the participants feel they can trust one another will determine the likelihood that any of the possible obstacles to effective deliberation must be faced. Any deliberation that deals with complex matters, scientific or otherwise, probably will require that a variety of information and expertise be made available to the participants. Whether the participants are randomly selected or are instead selected to represent specific interests in a policy dispute may affect how much attention will need to be paid to potential conflicts among the participants. Presumably, if the participants in the deliberation are randomly selected, there may be less need to deal with unexpressed emotions that may have developed over a protracted conflict involving specific policy disputes. On the other hand, depending on the subject matter of the deliberation, even if the participants are randomly selected, both negative attachments and positive commitments may still need to be openly discussed. If the participants themselves are adversaries in a particular dispute, then there is a greater chance that negative attachments and/or positive commitments will need to be discussed. Finally, if a common interest cannot be envisioned, if the power or skill differential among the parties is great, and if there seems to be no basis to promote trust among the participants, then these individuals are better off using an adversarial process for decision making that does not assume common interests, does not rely on consensus, and may not require face-to-face discussions.[77] The advantages and disadvantages of searching for common interests, not only in policy deliberations in the public sphere(s) and governmental sector(s), but in the attempt to develop or foster a realm of civil ethics, are revisited in chapter 6.

The next chapter analyzes a formal deliberation that arose out of a conflict over the siting of a hazardous waste landfill in Fort Wayne, Indiana. The chapter traces the political and regulatory context in which the dispute over the landfill emerged, the forces that shaped the context for a deliberative process to be utilized, the nature and outcomes of the deliberation that took place, and the unresolved issues that the community still faces.

NOTES

1. Seyla Benhabib, *The Reluctant Modernism of Hannah Arendt* (Thousand Oaks, Calif.: Sage, 1996), 200; see also 193–200.

2. Benjamin Barber, *A Place for Us: How to Make Society Civil and Democracy Strong* (New York: Hill and Wang, 1998); John Ehrenberg, *Civil Society: The Critical History of an Idea* (New York: New York University Press, 1999); Brian O'Connell, *Civil Society: The Underpinnings of Democracy* (Hanover, N.H.: University Press of New England, 1999); Robert D. Putnam, *Bowling Alone: The Collapse and Revival of American Community* (New York: Simon & Schuster, 2001).

3. See Robert N. Bellah et al., *Habits of the Heart: Individualism and Commitment in American Life* (Berkeley: University of California Press, 1985), viii, on the significance of this term used by Tocqueville.

4. John Stone and Stephen Mennell, eds., *Alexis de Tocqueville: On Democracy, Revolution, and Society* (Chicago: University of Chicago Press, 1980), 377.

5. Robert N. Bellah, *The Broken Covenant: American Civil Religion in Time of Trial*, 2nd ed. (Chicago: University of Chicago Press, 1992), 3.

6. Emile Durkheim, *The Elementary Forms of the Religious Life* (1915; reprint, New York: Free Press, 1965), 52–63.

7. Jürgen Habermas, *Between Facts and Norms: Contributions to a Discourse Theory of Law and Democracy*, trans. William Rehg (Cambridge, Mass.: MIT Press, 1996).

8. Bellah, *Broken Covenant*, 24

9. Jane Mansbridge, *Beyond Adversary Democracy* (Chicago: University of Chicago Press, 1983), viii.

10. Bellah, *Broken Covenant*, 53

11. Thomas E. Patterson, *We the People: A Concise Introduction to American Politics*, 4th ed. (New York: McGraw-Hill, 2002), A–A4.

12. Abraham Lincoln, "Address Delivered at the Dedication of the Cemetery at Gettysburg, November 19, 1863," *Great Speeches: Abraham Lincoln*, ed. John Grafton (New York: Dover, 1991), 103.

13. Lincoln, "Second Inaugural Address, March 4, 1865," 107.

14. Lincoln, "Second Inaugural," 107–108.

15. Grafton, ed., *Great Speeches*, 106.

16. Lincoln, "First Inaugural Address, March 4, 1861," italics mine.

17. Jody Rosen, "Two American Anthems, in Two American Voices," *New York Times*, 2 July 2000, Art and Leisure section, 1, 28; Celestine Bohlen, "No. 1 Anthem: 'God Bless America,'" *New York Times*, 19 September 2001, 1(E); Hal Leonard, *Irving Berlin's God Bless America and Other Songs for a Better Nation* (Milwaukee, Wis.: Hal Leonard, 2001), 80–81, 14–15, 35–39, 102–103; Jerry Silverman, *Of Thee I Sing: Lyrics and Music for America's Most Patriotic Songs* (New York: Kensington, 2002), 155–157, 158–160, 242–244.

18. On public sphere(s) and governmental sector(s), see Habermas, *Between Facts and Norms;* Craig Calhoun, ed., *Habermas and the Public Sphere* (Cambridge, Mass.: MIT Press, 1996); and Benhabib, *The Reluctant Modernism*, 193–220.

19. On public reasoning, see James Bohman and William Rehg, eds., *Deliberative Democracy: Essays on Reason and Politics* (Cambridge, Mass.: MIT Press, 1999); on "will formation," see Habermas, *Between Facts and Norms*.

20. On "opinion formation," see Habermas, *Between Facts and Norms*.

21. John Rawls, "The Idea of Public Reason," in *Deliberative Democracy*, ed. Bohman and Rehg, 93–141.

22. On "the good," see Michael Sandel, *Democracy's Discontent: America in Search of a Public Philosophy* (Cambridge, Mass.: Belknap Press of Harvard University Press, 1996), 3–24.

23. Sandel, *Democracy's Discontent*, 91–122.

24. The Dalai Lama, *Ethics for the New Millennium* (New York: Riverhead, 1999), 22. In his book the Dalai Lama also distinguishes between spirituality, which includes certain affirmative values and actions, and ethics, which refers to values according to which or actions by which one refrains from doing harm to another. As I describe the realm of civil ethics, I see both sets of values as relevant.

25. Edward O. Wilson, *The Future of Life* (New York: Knopf, 2002).

26. Habermas, *Between Facts and Norms*.

27. John Rawls, *Justice as Fairness: A Restatement*, ed. Erin Kelly (Cambridge, Mass.: Belknap Press of Harvard University Press, 2001).

28. Robert B. Westbrook, *John Dewey and American Democracy* (Ithaca, N.Y.: Cornell University Press, 1991), 49.

29. These process variables are similar to ones used by Benjamin Barber in *Strong Democracy: Participatory Politics for a New Age* (Berkeley: University of California Press, 1984), 261–311, when he analyzes the need to institutionalize "strong democratic talk," "strong democratic decision-making," and "strong democratic action."

30. Habermas, *Between Facts and Norms*, 329–387; Jürgen Habermas, "Popular Sovereignty as Procedure," in *Deliberative Democracy*, ed. James Bohman and William Rehg, 35–66.

31. See Steven Brint, "Gemeinschaft Revisited: A Critique and Reconstruction of the Community Concept," *Sociological Theory* 19, no. 1 (March 2001): 1–23.

32. Putnam, *Bowling Alone*, 19.

33. Sandel, *Democracy's Discontent*, 350.

34. Hannah Arendt, *The Human Condition* (Chicago: University of Chicago Press, 1998).

35. Rawls, *Justice as Fairness*, 11.

36. Habermas, *Between Facts and Norms*.

37. Benhabib, *Reluctant Modernism of Hannah Arendt*, 200.

38. Habermas, *Between Facts and Norms*.

39. On the meaning of *res publica* (literally, "the public thing"), see Robert A. Dahl, *On Democracy* (New Haven, Conn.: Yale University Press, 1998), 13, 16–17.

40. Habermas, *Between Facts and Norms*.

41. Mansbridge, *Beyond Adversary Democracy*.

42. Mansbridge, *Beyond Adversary Democracy*.

43. Habermas, *Between Facts and Norms*, 329–387.

44. Sandel, *Democracy's Discontent*, 3–122.

45. Sandel, *Democracy's Discontent*, 91–122.

46. See Linda Greenhouse, "The Competing Visions of the Role of the Court," *New York Times*, 7 July 2002, Week in Review section, 3.

47. John A. Hall and Charles Lindholm, *Is America Breaking Apart?* (Princeton, N.J.: Princeton University Press, 1999), 98.

48. Mansbridge, *Beyond Adversary Democracy*, 293.

49. Mansbridge, *Beyond Adversary Democracy*.

50. Robert K. Merton, *Social Theory and Social Structure* (New York: Free Press, 1968).

51. Putnam, *Bowling Alone*; Everett Carll Ladd, *The Ladd Report* (New York: Free Press, 1999).

52. Robert Wuthnow, *Loose Connections: Joining Together in America's Fragmented Communities* (Cambridge, Mass.: Harvard University Press, 1998).

53. Seyla Benhabib, "Models of Public Space: Hannah Arendt, the Liberal Tradition, and Jürgen Habermas," in *Habermas and the Public Sphere*, ed. Craig Calhoun (Cambridge, Mass.: MIT Press, 1996), 73–98; Habermas, "Popular Sovereignty as Procedure," 35–66; and Bohman and William Rehg, introduction to *Deliberative Democracy*, ed. Bohman and Rehg, ix–xxx.

54. Joshua Cohen, "Deliberation and Democratic Legitimacy," in *Deliberative Democracy*, ed. Bohman and Rehg, 77.

55. Bohman and Rehg, introduction to *Deliberative Democracy*, ed. Bohman and Rehg, ix–xxx.

56. Dorothy Nelkin and Michael Pollack, "Public Participation in Technological Decisions: Reality or Grand Illusion?" *Technology Review* 81, no. 8 (1979): 55–64; Nancy E. Abrams and Joel R. Primack, "The Public and Technological Decisions," *Bulletin of the Atomic Scientists* 6 (June 1980): 44–48; Mansbridge, *Beyond Adversary Democracy*; Robert Dahl, *Controlling Nuclear Weapons: Democracy versus Guardianship* (Syracuse, N.Y.: Syracuse University Press, 1985); Douglas J. Amy, "Environmental Dispute Resolution," in *Environmental Policy in the 1990s*, ed. Norman J. Vig and Michael E. Kraft (Washington, D.C.: Congressional Quarterly, 1990), 211–234; Roger Fisher and William Ury, *Getting to Yes: Negotiating Agreement without Giving In*, ed. Bruce Patton, 2nd ed. (New York: Penguin, 1991).

57. Mansbridge, *Beyond Adversary Democracy*, 255.

58. Tina Kelley, "Reginald Rose, 81, TV Writer Noted for 'Twelve Angry Men,'" *New York Times*, 21 April 2002, 40 (1).

59. Mansbridge, *Beyond Adversary Democracy*, vii–xiv, 3–38, 252–269.

60. Mansbridge, *Beyond Adversary Democracy*, 256.

61. Mansbridge, *Beyond Adversary Democracy*, 299–304.

62. Mansbridge argues that the American communes and collectives of the 1960s, although created as unitary systems, broke down from the weight of endless procedure, as the members, raised in an adversary democracy, insisted on equal power in all decisions (*Beyond Adversary Democracy*, vii–xiv, 233–251).

63. Mansbridge, *Beyond Adversary Democracy*, 233–251.

64. Habermas, *Between Facts and Norms*, 486; Bohman and William Rehg, introduction to *Deliberative Democracy*, ed. Bohman and Rehg, xv.

65. Dahl, *Controlling Nuclear Weapons*; James S. Fishkin, *Democracy and Deliberation: New Directions for Democratic Reform* (New Haven: Yale University Press, 1991); James S. Fishkin, *The Voice of the People: Public Opinion and Democracy* (New Haven: Yale University Press, 1995); Nancy E. Abrams and Joel R. Primack, "The Public and Technological Decisions."

66. Dahl, *Controlling Nuclear Weapons*.

67. See Jane Mansbridge, "A Deliberative Theory of Interest Group Representation," in *The Politics of Interests: Interest Groups Transformed*, ed. Mark P. Petracca (Boulder, Colo.: Westview, 1992), 32–57.

68. Dahl, *Controlling Nuclear Weapons*, 3.

69. Dahl, *Controlling Nuclear Weapons*, 88.

70. Fishkin, *Democracy and Deliberation*; Fishkin, *Voice of the People*.

71. Abrams and Primack, "The Public and Technological Decisions."

72. William D. Ruckelshaus, "Risk in a Free Society," *Environmental Law Reporter* 14 (1984): 1090–1094.

73. Abrams and Primack, "The Public and Technological Decisions," 46.

74. Mansbridge, *Beyond Adversary Democracy*, 25.

75. Rawls, "Idea of Public Reason," 93–141.

76. Fisher and Ury, *Getting to Yes*, 30.

77. Mansbridge, *Beyond Adversary Democracy*, 299–303.

3

Fostering Democratic Deliberation over Environmental Policy: The Indiana Hazardous Waste Facility Site Approval Authority

The method of democracy—insofar as it is that of organized intelligence—is to bring these conflicts [conflicting private and social interests] out into the open where their special claims can be seen and appraised, where they can be discussed and judged in the light of more inclusive interests than are represented by either of them separately.

—John Dewey, *Liberalism and Social Action*

INTRODUCTION

A mechanism for democratically deliberating about the future of a hazardous waste landfill in northeastern Indiana emerged almost by serendipity in June 1995.[1] The landfill's history actually began twenty-two years earlier, when the site was first considered for a solid waste (sanitary or "garbage") landfill in 1973. In March 1996, sixteen years after the solid waste landfill's owners first submitted permits to use the land as an exclu-

41

sively hazardous waste ("secure") landfill, the Indiana Hazardous Waste Facility Site Approval Authority (also referred to here as the "Siting Authority") denied the landfill a Certificate of Compatibility (CEC), preventing it from expanding beyond its then 151-acre site. Two years later, in June of 1998, the landfill officially closed. This chapter reviews the regulatory and political history of the landfill, the conditions under which the Indiana Hazardous Waste Facility Site Approval Authority was called into session, the proceedings and deliberations of the Siting Authority, and the implications of this deliberative mechanism for community, democracy, and the environment.

A HAZARDOUS WASTE LANDFILL COMES
TO NORTHEAST INDIANA

Until 1976, with the passage of the Resource Conservation and Recovery Act (RCRA, amended in 1984 and 1989), there was no distinction in federal law between solid waste (defined as any unwanted or discarded material that is not a liquid or gas) and hazardous waste, which has one or more of four characteristics: (1) it contains one of thirty-nine listed compounds in sufficient quantity to be toxic, carcinogenic, mutagenic, or teratogenic; (2) it is ignitible, such as gasoline; (3) it is reactive, such as ammonia; and (4) it is corrosive, such as industrial cleaning solvents.[2] That means that until 1976, solid wastes and hazardous wastes were generally disposed of together in unlined landfills that were not required to be monitored for leachates and groundwater contamination. This may help to explain why approximately one-fifth of Superfund sites in the United States are former municipal landfills.[3] It was of course the events surrounding an abandoned hazardous waste site in Love Canal, New York, in 1978, and the eventual federal response to them in 1981, that put the issue of hazardous wastes on the national policy agenda. While RCRA defined what hazardous wastes were, and how they should be transported and disposed of, it was the Comprehensive Environmental Response, Compensation, and Liability Act (CERCLA or Superfund, 1981, amended in 1986) that delineated how the nation would deal with existing hazardous waste sites that posed substantial threats to surrounding communities. There are approximately thirteen hundred such sites on the National Priorities List under Superfund, although studies have projected that between two thousand and ten thousand additional sites might qualify for inclusion.[4]

Fort Wayne (population 205,727) is the second largest city in Indiana, located approximately 120 miles north and east of the centrally situated state capital in Indianapolis. It is part of Allen County, a metropolitan region of 331,849. Also within the county, at Fort Wayne's eastern edge, is the city of New Haven (population 12,406).[5] Fort Wayne, founded at the confluence of three rivers, has been important to east-west transportation from the earliest fur-trapping days, through the time of canal construction, and still later, during the heyday of the railroads. The St. Joseph River and the St. Mary's River meet in Fort Wayne, forming the Maumee River, which flows east into Lake Erie and eventually into the Atlantic Ocean. The Wabash River, to the west of Fort Wayne, empties into the Mississippi River, the Gulf of Mexico, and the Pacific Ocean. These rivers made Fort Wayne significant historically as a portage site. The city and state remain important transportation routes, but now, of course, in the national highway system. This "centrality" of Indiana is reflected in the state's motto, "Crossroads of America."[6] As John Bartlow Martin observes:

> Here is Indiana, the central place, the crossroads, the mean that is sometimes golden, sometimes only mean. Consider the boundaries—Chicago, Ohio's steel cities and neat little farms, the Kentucky hills and bluegrass below the Ohio, Illinois and the westward sweep of the great prairies. Indiana is none of these, but it includes them all.[7]

While agriculture was important in the state—and in the northeast region—during the nineteenth and first half of the twentieth centuries, and is still important today, manufacturing became the dominant force in the Fort Wayne economy after World War II; in 2000, it still accounted for 21 percent of employment in Fort Wayne, almost 26 percent of employment in New Haven, and 22 percent of employment in Allen County.[8] Like other cities and regions in the United States that have been dependent on manufacturing, however, Fort Wayne and Allen County, in recent years, have sought to diversify their economic bases, and, to some extent, have done this with the emergence of financial, insurance, health, and other service-oriented sectors of the economy. In 2000, almost 20 percent of Fort Wayne's workforce was employed in education, health, and social services, while 16 percent of those in New Haven and 19 percent of those in Allen County were similarly employed.[9] Finance, insurance, real estate, professional, scientific, and waste management jobs comprised an additional 14 percent of employment in the area, while retail trade accounted for almost 13 percent of employment in the region.[10]

In 1999, the median household income was $36,518 in Fort Wayne, $41,802 in New Haven, and $42,671 in Allen County.[11] In 2000, over 17 percent of the residents in Fort Wayne were African American and almost 6 percent were Hispanic. In the same year, less than 1 percent of residents in New Haven were African American, while 2 percent were Hispanic; 11

percent of Allen County residents were African American and 4 percent were Hispanic.[12] The median home value in Fort Wayne in 2000 was $74,600; in New Haven, the median home value was $77,600, and in Allen County the median home value was $88,700. In 2000, almost 62 percent of Fort Wayne homes were owner occupied, while almost 80 percent of New Haven homes and 71 percent of Allen County homes were owner occupied.[13]

In 1973, a local waste hauler purchased two eighty-acre farms in an unincorporated part of Allen County with the intention of opening a sanitary landfill. The land was situated between the cities of Fort Wayne and New Haven. Though within the county, the land came under the planning jurisdiction of Fort Wayne. The land had been zoned I-3 (heavy industrial); local planners apparently were hoping that some outlying portions of the county, particularly those near rail lines, might prove attractive for economic development. The Fort Wayne I-3 designation meant a landfill could not be developed there without a public hearing and a special exception. At a public hearing held in December 1973, nearby residents expressed strong opposition to the landfill's development. Following this, the Fort Wayne Board of Zoning Appeals turned down the request for a special exception.[14]

In April 1974, jurisdiction for zoning in unincorporated portions of the county reverted to Allen County. The local waste hauler then asked the county planning administrator to clarify what "open land uses" meant under the county's I-3 zoning designation. In response, the planning administrator amended the zoning rules to specifically allow "dumps and landfills" on I-3 zoned land. The county commissioners approved this change to the zoning ordinances in June 1974. However, by July 1974, the commissioners were having second thoughts. According to some residents, the commissioners probably wanted to develop a new sanitary landfill at the proposed site on Adams Center Road; however, they did not intend that *any* I-3 zoned property in the county could be turned into a "dump or landfill" without a special exception. So, in July 1974, the commissioners voted to amend the county zoning ordinances again. This time they approved a rule that specifically outlawed landfills on I-3 zoned land without a special exception. However, this new zoning rule would not take effect until August 31, 1974. The local waste hauler then submitted his application for a sanitary landfill on Adams Center Road in mid-July 1974.[15]

Though not required, a public hearing on the sanitary landfill request was held in August 1974. A majority of the two hundred people attending the hearing, as well as sixteen hundred people who had signed a petition, expressed strong opposition to the landfill's development. The matter then came before the Allen County Board of Zoning Appeals. The board members, "with great reluctance," approved the landfill's development because, as the board chair noted, "we have no legal choice." The board members, though concerned about the absence of any analysis of the landfill's impacts on the local community, concluded that a landfill was a "permitted use" of that property at the time the landfill petition was received in July 1974.[16]

The landfill received a construction permit from the state and an operating permit from the Indiana Stream Pollution Control Board in 1975. The Indiana Stream Pollution Control Board was part of the Indiana State Board of Health; it had jurisdiction over certain environmental matters until the Indiana Department of Environmental Management (IDEM) was created in 1985. A sanitary landfill thus began operating on Adams Center Road in Allen County, Indiana, in 1975. However, with the passage of the Resource Conservation and Recovery Act in 1976, states were required to develop their own plans for the safe disposal of hazardous wastes. The Indiana State Board of Health notified solid waste landfill operators that if they were receiving any of the wastes now listed as hazardous under RCRA, they must create a separate site for disposing of those wastes. Soon after, the operator of the Adams Center Landfill opened a new, unlined cell for hazardous wastes to the east of the eighty acres he was using for the disposal of solid wastes.[17]

In 1980, the Adams Center Landfill was sold to a national waste management firm, the Sanitation Corporation of America (SCA). Shortly thereafter, the U.S. Environmental Protection Agency (EPA) issued guidelines, under RCRA, defining the criteria for developing federally licensed hazardous waste landfills. The EPA invited any existing sanitary landfill operators to indicate their interest in dealing exclusively with hazardous waste by submitting a Part A permit under RCRA. SCA did this in 1980. When the State of Indiana passed its Hazardous Waste Program in 1980, in conformance with RCRA, the Adams Center Landfill also received state permission to begin developing a hazardous waste landfill at the site.[18]

No neighbors near the landfill, nor for that matter any county residents, were notified of the landfill's changing status. The landfill operators were not required by federal or state law to notify residents. However, county residents who had used the landfill were aware that something about the landfill was changing; they were now being turned away from the landfill with building materials and other solid wastes that the landfill had previously accepted. Michael Edelstein calls this period in community disputes over hazardous waste issues the "incubation" or "pre-disaster stage." There may be indications of "trouble up ahead," yet it is easier to act as though nothing worthy of worry is going on.[19]

In late 1984, the landfill was purchased by Chemical Waste Management, Incorporated, a subsidiary of Waste Management, Incorporated, at the time, one of the largest corporations in the United States and a major player in the field of waste management. Two years later, Chemical Waste Management purchased an additional two hundred acres east of the original 151-acre landfill site on Adams Center Road. The company also began the process of applying for a Part B (permanent operating) permit to operate a fully licensed federal hazardous waste landfill on the site of the original landfill. In 1988, four significant events in the landfill's history occurred. First, in early 1988, a group of concerned citizens formed the Allen County Dump Stoppers; they learned the landfill was in the final stages of being approved for its Part B permit. Edelstein notes that often, not until there is some official announcement regarding a contaminated site (or in this case, a site to hold contaminated wastes) is there a formal, organized response by community residents. The Dump Stoppers' goal was to prevent Chemical Waste Management from obtaining its Part B permit for the Adams Center Landfill and to prevent it from expanding across Adams Center Road.[20]

Second, in March 1988, the Indiana Department of Environmental Management announced that it had tentatively approved a Part B permit for the Adams Center Landfill. The landfill now consisted of four hazardous waste cells, with the first cell (Phase I) unlined, as was the now closed sanitary landfill; Phases II and III with a single-liner system; and Phase IV with a "state-of-the-art" double liner and leachate system. The cells were now also being monitored for groundwater contamination. Before the actual hearing on the Part B permit, Chemical Waste Management withdrew Phase IV from the permit request. IDEM announced it would hold a public hearing in May 1988 to receive comments on the landfill's permit application.[21]

Third, more than six hundred people attended a joint IDEM/EPA hearing on the Part B permit for Adams Center Landfill in a New Haven high school in May 1988. The landfill was geographically closer to the city of New Haven than to the city of Fort Wayne, and many of the leaders and members of the Dump Stoppers lived in New Haven or unincorporated sections of Allen County. While New Haven is predominantly a white, working-class community, the census tracts closest to the proposed landfill site generally had lower household incomes than other parts of New Haven. The census tracts to the west of the landfill in the city of Fort Wayne were predominantly African American, with among the lowest household incomes in the city of Fort Wayne.[22]

There was palpable anger and fear as the residents of Allen County rose to the microphone to express their concerns about the landfill. The speakers, for the most part, addressed what Krimsky and Plough[23] have called "cultural issues of risk." They were concerned about the landfill's impacts on the health of their children and other community residents, on the value of their homes, and on the future of their community. The EPA and IDEM representatives, however, were constrained to recording and responding to "technical issues of risk"; these consisted of statistical probabilities of harm posed by the landfill in terms of its structure and functioning. Edelstein[24] and others have noted that an element of the grievances felt by communities facing potential risks is the fact that community residents, on the one hand, and government officials, scientific experts, and corporate managers, on the other, speak in different languages about the risks posed. Interestingly, however, such experts may become equally concerned about cultural issues of risk when they, or their families, or their own communities are the potential victims of exposure.[25] Nonetheless, most federal and state public hearings about risks from potentially harmful pollutants pay almost no attention to the social, economic, psychological, or cultural impacts on a community.[26] In fact, several years after this public hearing held by IDEM and the EPA in May 1988, it became crystal clear that IDEM and the EPA were *not* concerned about the landfill's location at all. The EPA and IDEM considered the actual site of the landfill to be an issue for local zoning; they were concerned solely with whether the landfill could meet the technical construction and operating criteria established by RCRA.[27] Last, in September 1988, the Adams Center Landfill received its Part B permit, making it one of twenty-one federally licensed hazardous waste landfills in the United States and the only one in the state of Indiana.[28]

In May 1991, Chemical Waste Management announced its intention to seek a Part B permit for the two-hundred-acre site it had purchased across Adams Center Road. In February 1992, the city of Fort Wayne, preempting the city of New Haven, entered into an agreement with Chemical Waste Management to annex the Adams Center Hazardous Waste Landfill, as well as adjoining property to the south and east. No public hearing about the annexation was held, since this was considered a voluntary annexation, the necessary percentage of property owners having requested it. The petitioners included Chemical Waste Management itself, another corporation formed by Chemical Waste Management shortly before the annexation, and another corporation with representatives on the Board of Directors of Waste Management, Incorporated. Complicating the scenario further, one of Chemical Waste Management's lawyers was a member of the Fort Wayne City Council. Although he did not vote on the annexation, opponents of the landfill believed that he had played a key role in structuring the annexation agreement between the city of Fort Wayne and Chemical Waste Management. Financial terms included "tipping fees" to the city for every ton of hazardous waste buried in the landfill and a special redevelopment fund for the southeast section of Fort Wayne, the largely poor and minority area closest to the landfill. The annexation would not become effective until January 1, 2000. At that time, the landfill, like other businesses in the city, would pay property and income taxes. Critics of the annexation argued, however, that until the annexation took place, the city of Fort Wayne would be a financial beneficiary of the landfill, would have a direct interest in the landfill's expansion, and might conceivably be liable in any legal actions against the landfill for damages incurred from its operations. It appeared that little long-term analysis had been undertaken to examine the economic and environmental consequences of annexing the landfill into the city of Fort Wayne.[29]

As a result of the strong public outcry at the lack of a public hearing before the annexation took place, a public meeting was held after the annexation was approved. The anger and indignation expressed at this meeting prompted the mayor of Fort Wayne to appoint a Citizens' Commission on Hazardous Waste to study the landfill's impacts on the city and to make a recommendation about future landfill expansions. The commission members were given no funding to bring in expert witnesses or to hire independent staff. The person assigned by the mayor to assist the commission later left the city's employ to become the community relations director for the Adams Center Hazardous Waste Landfill. The commission relied heavily on data from Chemical Waste Management in its discussions. After meeting for almost two years, the members of the commission were asked by Fort Wayne's mayor to make a recommendation about landfill expansion. Some members of the commission objected, arguing that they lacked sufficient information or expertise to make such a recommendation. When the commission was pressed by the mayor to make a recommendation nonetheless and told it could not issue a minority report, two of its members resigned: one was a member of Dump Stoppers and the other a Fort Wayne City Council member who represented the southeast district of Fort Wayne that bordered the landfill. The remaining members of the commission "individually" endorsed a recommendation that the landfill be allowed to expand; no formal vote was taken, although originally a secret ballot had been proposed.[30]

Soon after the city of Fort Wayne, in February 1992, entered into its agreement to annex the Adams Center Hazardous Waste Landfill, the city of New Haven began a legal strategy to try to prevent the landfill's Phase IV from becoming operative and to deny Chemical Waste Management the ability to expand across Adams Center Road and open its proposed Phases V, VI, and VII. The legal approach undertaken by the city of New Haven meant that the city, not particularly affluent to begin with, would now be investing considerable money and other resources in the effort to stop the landfill's growth. This issue was faced openly by the mayor of New Haven, in consultation with the members of the city council, and with the support of a majority of New Haven residents. This decision became very significant because, without the willingness of the city of New Haven to engage in a legal struggle with Chemical Waste Management, the city of Fort Wayne, and Allen County, it is unlikely that the Indiana Hazardous Waste Facility Site Approval Authority would have been called into session in late 1995 to deliberate the future of the Adams Center Hazardous Waste Landfill.

In February 1993, the city of New Haven brought suit, in Allen County Superior Court, against Chemical Waste Management of Indiana, the Allen County Board of Zoning Appeals, the Indiana Department of Environmental Management, and the Indiana Hazardous Waste Facility Site Approval Authority.[31] The lawsuit contended that the Adams Center Hazardous Waste Landfill had never undergone a land-use or zoning review. The original sanitary landfill had not been subject to a zoning review because this use of the site had been permitted, although debated, when the landfill application was received in July 1974. After August 31, 1974, however, the reamended Allen County zoning ordinances required a special exception for the construction of a landfill on I-3 zoned property. When Chemical Waste Management began the process of applying for its Part B permit to operate a licensed hazardous waste landfill in 1986, there still was no zoning review by Allen County. Another option available for hazardous waste facility site review also was not utilized in 1986. The Indiana Hazardous Waste Facility Site Approval Authority had been created by the Indiana legislature in May 1981, as part of the state's hazardous waste program. Its purpose was to:

(1) provide for effective public participation in the siting process for hazardous waste facilities and low level radioactive waste facilities; (2) ensure that the impacts of hazardous waste facilities and low level radioactive facilities on communities are addressed and weighed against the public need for such a facility in a state; and (3) encourage technologies which (a) provide safe and effective alternatives to permanent entombment of hazardous wastes and low level radioactive wastes; or (b) reduce the volume or degree of hazard of those wastes which must be permanently entombed.[32]

The Siting Authority was to have a nine-member board, with five members appointed by the governor and four appointed by local officials in the jurisdiction(s) closest to the site under review.

The Siting Authority was not convened to review the Adams Center Hazardous Waste Landfill in 1986 because of a decision made by the commissioner of the Indiana Department of Environmental Management. Soon after Chemical Waste Management began the process of applying for its Part B permit in 1986, the executive director of the Siting Authority wrote to the commissioner of IDEM to inquire why the Siting Authority was not being called into session, since the Siting Authority had been given the responsibility to "certif[y] that a [hazardous waste or low level radioactive waste] facility presents no unacceptable environmental risk."[33] The commissioner of IDEM replied that there was no need for the Siting Authority to meet, because this was not a new landfill, but, rather, a landfill whose owners had received its original permits in 1974 and 1975 (before the Siting Authority was created) and then had legally amended those permits to operate a hazardous waste landfill (again, before the Siting Authority was created).[34] The opponents of the landfill (as well as many local officials) did not fully understand the import of the Siting Authority or of the decision made by the commissioner in 1986 until the issues were brought clearly into the light by the New Haven lawsuit. Local citizens went to the 1988 IDEM/EPA public hearing to present their concerns about the impacts the landfill might have on their community, only to discover that these agencies had not been created to examine such impacts. On the other hand, the body that was designed to have that review responsibility was told there was no reason for it to meet.

In August 1994, the judge in the suit brought by the city of New Haven issued a preliminary ruling that largely upheld the arguments made by New Haven. He ruled that the landfill was a "nonconforming use of the property," and that any expansion of the Adams Center Hazardous Waste Landfill must be approved either by the Allen County Board of Zoning Appeals (through its issuance of a special exception) or by the Indiana Hazardous Waste Facility Site Approval Authority (through its issuance of a Certificate of Environmental Compatibility). The only question left open by the judge was whether Phase IV, the hazardous waste cell under construction on the original landfill site, but withdrawn from the Part B permit in 1988, had to go before either Allen County Zoning or the state Siting Authority in order for it to be legally permitted. He indicated that Chemical Waste Management might be able to seek a jury trial to determine whether the "county's longstanding silence on the matter amounts to an implicit authorization of continued growth on the original 151-acre site."[35]

In September 1994, the Allen County Zoning Administrator issued two stop-work orders to halt construction of Phase IV of the Adams Center Hazardous Waste Landfill. County officials admitted that until the lawsuit brought by the city of New Haven, they believed they had no zoning jurisdiction over the landfill; they mistakenly thought the landfill had received its Certificate of Environmental Compatibility from the state Siting Authority.[36] In November 1994, the judge in the suit ruled that, while Allen County had the right to enforce certain restrictive (land-use) covenants that were agreed to when the sanitary landfill received its permit in

1974, Allen County could not stop the construction of Phase IV, since it was part of the original 151-acre site approved for a landfill in 1974. Any proposal to expand the landfill beyond the original 151-acre site, however, would have to go before the Allen County Board of Zoning Appeals or the Indiana Hazardous Waste Facility Site Approval Authority, as well as the Indiana Department of Environmental Management and the U.S. Environmental Protection Agency.[37]

The issuance of the two stop-work orders in September 1994 and six additional stop-work orders in February 1995 by the Allen County Zoning Administrator, based on the 1974 restrictive covenants, did not stop construction of Phase IV. Chemical Waste Management challenged the validity of the stop-work orders both before the Allen County Board of Zoning Appeals and in DeKalb County (Indiana) Circuit Court. Despite an effort by Chemical Waste Management to work out an agreement behind closed doors with the Allen County Board of Zoning Appeals to drop the stop-work orders, a strong public outcry forced the Allen County Board of Zoning Appeals to hold a public hearing on the validity of the Zoning Administrator's issuance of the stop-work orders. In a packed Allen County Common Council conference room in May 1995, after members of the public presented testimony, the Board of Zoning Appeals upheld the right of the Allen County Zoning Administrator to issue the stop-work orders.

The realization that Allen County might not be as hospitable to the operations of Chemical Waste Management as it had been in the past, the need for further landfill space (Phase IV involved only a 9.5-acre cell near the old sanitary landfill) and the judge's decision that any expansion of the Adams Center Hazardous Waste Landfill beyond the original 151-acre site must be approved either by the Allen County Board of Zoning Appeals or the Indiana Hazardous Waste Facility Site Approval Authority may have prompted Chemical Waste Management to go to the Indiana Hazardous Waste Facility Site Approval Authority to seek permission to expand the landfill. The Siting Authority was a largely untested mechanism; no other significant hazardous or low-level radioactive waste facility existed in the state. Chemical Waste Management submitted a proposal to the Siting Authority in June 1995 for a fifty-four-acre landfill on the 200 acres east of Adams Center Road (Phases V, VI, and VII) and a thirty-two-acre landfill on eighty acres west of the sanitary landfill (Phase VIII).[38] However, before Chemical Waste Management submitted its application to the Siting Authority, the Indiana legislature made two changes to the Siting Authority statute. Opponents of the landfill claimed that, despite Chemical Waste Management's declining influence in Allen County, it was still an important and strong lobbying presence in the state capital, particularly in making the argument that economic growth would be enhanced by having a federally licensed hazardous waste landfill in the state. The changes made to the Siting Authority statute involved a new adjudicatory phase of the Siting Authority deliberations and the phasing out of the Siting Authority after July 1, 1996.

THE INDIANA HAZARDOUS WASTE FACILITY
SITE APPROVAL AUTHORITY CONVENES
IN ALLEN COUNTY

The statute creating the Indiana Siting Authority authorized the governor to select its five statewide members. They were to be residents of the state "recognized around the state for their judgment, integrity and credibility." One was to represent business and industry, one labor, and one agriculture. The fourth statewide member was required to be a hydrogeologist who had practiced within the state for at least five years; the fifth member was to be a biologist, chemist, limnologist, or toxicologist who was either a faculty member of an institution of higher learning in the state or a scientist on the staff of an independent research institution in the state.[39] Two local members were to be appointed by the Allen County commissioners, the third local member would be selected by the mayor of New Haven, and the fourth local member by the mayor of Fort Wayne. By early December 1994, all nine members of the Siting Authority had been appointed. The statewide member chosen as a representative of business served as the Siting Authority presiding officer; she was involved in solid waste management and planning. The representative of labor was associated with the United Auto Workers, while the agricultural representative was employed by a major regional electric power producer. Both the hydrogeologist and the chemist appointed to the Siting Authority were faculty members at Purdue University in West Lafayette, Indiana. The Allen County commissioners chose an economics professor from Indiana University–Purdue University, Fort Wayne, and a small business owner from Fort Wayne as their two appointees. The mayor of New Haven chose a former member of the New Haven City Council, who was also a leader of a local labor federation, as his appointee, while the mayor of Fort Wayne chose a local physician.

Before any public hearings were held, Chemical Waste Management challenged the appointment made by the city of New Haven, arguing that the individual selected was biased because of public stances he had taken against the landfill's expansion. The mayor of New Haven responded that he had selected this individual because he was able to represent the views of New Haven. The members of the Siting Authority voted not to remove the New Haven delegate. However, by mid-March, the New Haven representative voluntarily resigned, saying that he did not want to become an issue in any possible court challenge to the Siting Authority's final decision. He was replaced by a small business owner from New Haven.[40]

The first public hearing of the Siting Authority took place in a public school in New Haven on January 20, 1996. The nine Siting Authority members sat at the front of the school's auditorium, facing over six hundred people, who filled the auditorium to standing-room-only capacity. The hearing lasted from 9:30 A.M. to 8 P.M.[41] The overwhelming majority of speakers presented arguments against the landfill's expansion. Having argued their case, in some instances, for over eight years, they made a series of systematic arguments about the problems posed by the landfill; these included the troubled history of decision making over the landfill, concerns about the landfill's potential impacts on groundwater and air, the possibility of hazardous waste trucks getting into accidents, especially with school buses, the decline in local property values, the stress on families and the community, and the cloud over the area's future. Representing a sea change in local political opinion, an array of elected officials also spoke against the landfill's expansion; they included the Allen County commissioners, members of the Allen County Council, state legislative representatives, and the local U.S. congressman. The only people speaking in favor of the landfill's expansion were employees of the landfill, consultants hired to analyze the economic benefits of the landfill, a representative of the mayor of Fort Wayne, a Fort Wayne City Council representative—elected after the death of the southeast Fort Wayne representative, who had been a strong critic of the landfill—and the Fort Wayne Interdenominational Ministerial Alliance. The hearing was long and intense, but orderly, courteous, and civil. One Siting Authority member commented, after the Siting Authority's vote on the request for a Certificate of Environmental Compatibility in March 1996, that the members of the Siting Authority had been strongly affected by the public testimony on that first day. For the statewide members, who knew almost nothing about the landfill's history and development, and even for the local members, a complex picture emerged, involving questions of economic growth, environmental protection, and fairness.

Following the public hearing, there was an additional two-week period in which anyone could submit written comments to the Siting Authority for review. The Siting Authority also received a report from an independent consultant who had been hired to look at, among other things, the economic and environmental impacts of the landfill; following the submission of the consultant's report, the public was permitted to offer written comments about it. The adjudicatory hearing was scheduled for March 19 to 21, 1996. In early March, despite objections from the lawyers for the city of New Haven, Chemical Waste Management received permission from the Siting Authority to amend its application; it withdrew Phases V, VI, and VII (the landfill proposed east of Adams Center Road) from consideration for a CEC.[42]

On each of the three days scheduled for the adjudicatory hearing in the Allen County Commissioners' Courtroom, the sessions began early in the day and ran late into the evening. Both the proponents and the opponents of Chemical Waste Management's application introduced expert witnesses, although the burden of proof remained on the proponents.[43] Each side called witnesses who first answered questions of the lawyers on the side for which they were testifying and then were cross-examined by the lawyers on the opposing side. Following this, the Siting Authority members asked questions of the witnesses. Witnesses were called to present testimony about the geology of the landfill site, the functioning of the landfill, the potential impacts of the landfill on groundwater and air, the impacts of transporting hazardous waste in the area, the risk of fire or explosion from the storage and treatment of hazardous waste on the site, the impact of the landfill on local property values, the availability of other hazardous and special waste landfills in the region, the economic benefits of the landfill, and the impact of the landfill on social trust and environmental equity. On March 21, the third day of the hearing, the testimony continued until 11 P.M. Once all the designated witnesses had been called, the presiding officer of the Siting Authority announced that the hearing of witnesses was officially concluded. She then announced that the members of the Siting Authority would begin its deliberations, that the deliberations would take place entirely in public view, but that no comments, questions, or interruptions would be permitted from those viewing the deliberations. She indicated that the Siting Authority would deliberate to a conclusion, if possible, that evening. One member of the Siting Authority said he was prepared to deliberate through the night, but would have to leave by 6 A.M. to make it on time to his job in another county. This drew polite laughter from the Siting Authority members, as well as the spectators, who perhaps wondered whether they could deliberate that long after a meeting schedule that had begun at 8:30 that morning. In fact, the deliberations lasted until 4:00 on the morning of March 22, 1996.

The statute that had created the Siting Authority provided no guidance about how final deliberations should be structured. Siting Authority members later explained that they had made the decision to conduct their deliberations in public during one of their breaks. They wanted to ensure that the public would fully understand what they had considered during their discussions. They did not want to provide an opportunity, or the appearance of an opportunity, for any party to the conflict to have access to the Siting Authority members, once all the evidence had been presented. They thus embarked on a deliberation, in front of about forty spectators, in the early morning hours preceding dawn.

The members of the Siting Authority went through the criteria that the statute set out for granting a Certificate of Environmental Compatibility. They reviewed the findings of fact and conclusions of law they would have to address. And then they began to look at the testimony and evidence that had been presented to them in the last two months. As an issue came up, it was addressed from several perspectives, it was turned over, it was examined in detail. The nine members of the Siting Authority quietly discussed the various facets of the landfill's existence: its location above particular aquifers that expert witnesses had testified about, the functioning of liners and leachate systems, the ability to monitor air pollution, the impact on property values, the availability of other landfills that could take hazardous or special waste in the region. They talked to each other and they listened to each other. They displayed the elements that Mansbridge[44] has described as characterizing the unitary form of democracy: the assumption of a common interest, the stance of mutual respect, the process of making a decision face-to-face, and the effort to reach a consensus. At about 4 A.M., they voted. By a margin of eight to one, they decided to deny Chemical Waste Management its request for a Certificate of Environmental Compatibility for Phase VIII. The representative of labor was the only Siting Authority member not in agreement with that resolution. The formal findings of fact and conclusions of law would not be issued until May 7, 1996. On that night, however, the basis for the majority's decision emerged. First and foremost, they were concerned about the landfill's proximity to critical and vulnerable aquifers. The hydrogeologist on the panel observed that the site "was not a very good choice for a landfill." He was concerned about the complexity of the land under the landfill, the difficulty of finding and ameliorating any leaks, and the absence of models that would help in uncovering the direction that contaminants would actually move if released.[45] He noted that America has two key natural resources: water and soil. It is incumbent on us to take care of them, he argued, since the prospect of global warming would make maintaining the integrity of groundwater ever more urgent.

The members of the authority were also concerned about a risk assessment that Chemical Waste Management had introduced into evidence to evaluate the likelihood of harm coming to those living near the landfill. The professor of economics appointed by Allen County commented, "I never heard a number, but I heard, 'We'll be OK.' I felt more uncomfortable after the presentation than before it began." This same authority member also thought that the study introduced by Chemical Waste Management to assess the impact of the landfill on nearby property values was poorly designed and implemented. He observed, "Given the amount of money spent by the applicant, it's truly a shame those hypotheses were not researched [adequately]." The chemist on the panel noted that a survey introduced into evidence by the opponents of landfill expansion had indicated that about 70 percent of Allen County residents were opposed to the landfill's receiving a CEC. He then concluded, "The city government, the city council must want it. They entered into an agreement to annex it. Fort Wayne must love it."[46] This same panel member also noted, "It is not a question of will the liners leak, but when." Members of the Siting Authority also discussed the idea that one of their charges was to promote alternatives to the storing of hazardous waste in the ground. They concluded that if landfills like Adams Center were allowed to expand ad infinitum, there would be no incentive to change production processes or to develop alternatives to landfills. The Siting Authority members also considered the fact that at least one other landfill in central Indiana, which was permitted to take "special waste," could fill some of the vacuum left by Chemical Waste Management. While some waste generators might feel more comfortable putting their "special waste" in a federally designated "secure" landfill, reasoning it might better protect them from potential liability under Superfund, they could nonetheless utilize this other site in the state, as well as secure landfills in other states. The presiding officer may have well summed up much of what the other panel members were feeling when she said, "I think it would be irresponsible of us to put a hazardous waste facility on an improper site."[47]

On April 10, 1996, the Siting Authority again met in Fort Wayne. It rejected Chemical Waste Management's request for another hearing on its landfill proposal and a petition to remove two members of the Siting Authority for bias. The Siting Authority concluded that Chemical Waste Management had adequate recourse in the courts if it wanted to pursue a new hearing. The authority members also believed there was no basis to doubt the fairness or objectivity of the two members called into question by Chemical Waste Management. One was the small business owner appointed by Allen County; Chemical Waste Management claimed that he was biased because he had signed a petition against the landfill's expansion in 1995, when the validity of the stop-work orders came before the Allen County Board of Zoning Appeals. The member in question said that he didn't remember signing the petition, but when given the opportunity to review it he observed, "As I reread it, it was the motherhood-and-apple pie thing. My recollection is they [the petitioners] were saying Chem Waste should follow the law. And I am a person who thinks everybody, including the landfill, should follow the law, and that, I'm sure is the reason I signed it."[48] The other member of the Siting Authority challenged by Chemical Waste Management was the second individual appointed by the city of New Haven. Chemical Waste Management said that he was biased because he lived close enough to the landfill to be financially affected by the outcome of the Siting Authority's decision. The Siting Authority members denied both claims of bias, and they also unanimously adopted the findings of fact that would become part of their final report on Chemical Waste Management's CEC request.[49]

The Siting Authority issued its "Findings of Fact, Conclusions of Law and Final Order Regarding the Application for a CEC Submitted by Chemical Waste Management of Indiana, L.L.C." on May 7, 1996. The members of the authority determined that, "based upon the hydrogeological characteristics of the site, the groundwater of Allen County is threatened by the proposed Phase 8. The risk and probable impact of contamination of groundwater is a sufficient basis for denial." Additionally, they noted, "In light of the dangers posed by siting the facility on the proposed property, the potential long-term liability and the short-term negative impacts outweigh the economic benefits derived from fees, taxes, and jobs." And they concluded, "Combining the risks of groundwater contamination and all other impacts of the proposed facility, the potential costs posed by this facility are greater than the potential benefits derived by the public."[50] Soon after, Chemical Waste Management sued the Indiana Hazardous Waste Facility Site Approval Authority in Marion County (Indianapolis) Superior Court. The suit claimed the Siting Authority decision was flawed because of the two members of the authority that Chemical Waste Management maintained were biased and because of a host of other problems the suit argued marred the Siting Authority hearings, deliberations, findings, and conclusions.

In July 1996, Chemical Waste Management settled its lawsuit with Allen County regarding the stop-work orders and the restrictive land-use covenants. The city of New Haven was not party to those discussions and initiated its own lawsuits, first against Allen County for excluding it from those negotiations and then against Chemical Waste Management and Allen County for what the city of New Haven believed were ongoing violations of several of the 1974 covenants. Although New Haven's challenge to the Allen County Board of Zoning Appeals for excluding it from negotiations was eventually dismissed, the suit challenging that Chemical Waste Management was in violation of some of the 1974 restrictive covenants proceeded, with a trial date set for the end of 2002.[51] Meanwhile, in late 1996, the Fort Wayne City Council voted to move up the date for annexing the landfill. Originally set for January 1, 2000, the annexation would now become effective in early 1997. Opponents of the landfill's expansion feared that Chemical Waste Management might try to work around the Siting Authority's ruling by seeking permission for a new site that would now be within the zoning jurisdiction of Fort Wayne. And, in fact, in May 1997, Chemical Waste Management submitted to the Fort

Wayne Board of Zoning Appeals a proposal to open a new Phase X, east of Adams Center Road, consisting of twenty-four acres on the parcel of land just east of the site it had dropped from its landfill application (Phases V, VI, and VII) before the Siting Authority in March 1996.[52] However, in June 1997, Chemical Waste Management lost a significant public relations battle when the Indiana Department of Environmental Management found that Chemical Waste Management had failed to pass the state's "Good Character Review" in its quest to lengthen the slopes of Phase IV, the only operating hazardous waste cell at the landfill. The IDEM ruling concluded: "There is a history of repeated violations of state and federal environmental laws among Chem Waste, its subsidiaries and their affiliates. A reasonable inference from this pattern of conduct is that some of the violations were knowing violations."[53]

On October 13, 1997, Chemical Waste Management announced that it was withdrawing its application for the newly proposed Phase X from consideration before IDEM. A week later, the judge in Marion County who had heard the suit brought by Chemical Waste Management against the Indiana Hazardous Waste Facility Site Approval Authority ruled that the Siting Authority decision was "tainted" because of the Allen County appointee who had signed the petition against the landfill. The judge stated that "an objective person familiar with the circumstances 'would have a reasonable basis for doubting [the Siting Authority member's] impartiality.' "[54] Chemical Waste Management asked the judge to void the Siting Authority's decision, but in a ruling two weeks later, the judge returned the case to the Indiana Hazardous Waste Facility Site Approval Authority "for further proceeding."[55] On November 25, 1997, the office of the Indiana Attorney General filed a notice indicating it would appeal the decision of the Marion County judge on behalf of the Siting Authority. Then, on the very same day, Chemical Waste Management announced that it would suspend operations at the Adams Center Landfill in mid-1998.[56] The landfill received its last load of waste in late May 1998.[57] The landfill had been unsuccessful in expanding beyond the original 151-acre site acquired by Chemical Waste Management in 1984, and new market forces, the disclosure of questionable accounting practices in its parent company, the departure of Waste Management's CEO, and the 20 percent drop in its stock price in late October 1997 all may have played a part in the decision to suspend operations at Adams Center.[58]

THE SIGNIFICANCE OF THE SITING AUTHORITY

As a mechanism for dealing with a protracted conflict over a significant environmental issue, the Indiana Hazardous Waste Facility Site Approval

Authority had much to commend it. Still, its usefulness in fostering democratic deliberation over the Adams Center Hazardous Waste Landfill might have been limited if a balance of power had not been achieved by the contending interests over the years of the dispute. Douglas Amy[59] notes that such a balance of power is one among several conditions necessary for "environmental dispute resolution" processes to work. The Siting Authority should have been called into session in 1986, when Chemical Waste Management began the process of applying for its final Part B operating permit. It did not meet because the executive director of the Indiana Department of Environmental Management ruled that the landfill was not a new facility, but one that had originally received its permit in 1974 and had subsequently legally amended it. This ruling was issued despite the fact that, after September 1, 1974, any new landfill in Allen County required a special exception, which Adams Center Landfill had never received, and that after 1980, Adams Center was no longer a sanitary landfill, but was in the process of becoming an exclusively hazardous waste landfill.

Yet, if the Siting Authority had met in 1986, the opponents of the landfill would have been poorly organized and poorly prepared to take on the task of convincing the Siting Authority members that this was not a good location for a hazardous waste landfill. It was not until 1988, with the announcement by IDEM that it had tentatively approved a Part B permit for Adams Center Landfill, that a well-functioning, community-based, citizen organization formed to oppose the Part B permit for Adams Center Landfill. And it was not until 1991, when Chemical Waste Management announced plans to submit an application for a Part B permit for two hundred acres to the east of Adams Center Road, that a new, stronger, and more effective group of leaders took the helm of the Allen County Dump Stoppers. The new leaders spent untold hours researching the history of decisions made about the landfill and examining the multitudinous impacts the facility was having and likely would continue to have on the community. The new leadership was productive in expanding the base of the organization's members. And the new leaders worked closely with the mayor of New Haven and the New Haven City Council to develop the lawsuit in early 1993 against Chemical Waste Management, Allen County, the city of Fort Wayne, and the Indiana Hazardous Waste Facility Site Approval Authority. It was the judge's decision in that case in August 1994 and the sudden realization by Allen County that it did have zoning jurisdiction over the landfill that set in motion the chain of events that led to Chemical Waste Management applying for a Certificate of Environmental Compatibility from the Indiana Hazardous Waste Facility Site Approval Authority. Moreover, the changes made to the Siting Authority statute at the urging of Chemical Waste Management in June 1995, particularly the addition of an adjudicatory phase to the Siting Authority proceedings, may have provided the landfill's opponents with a potent opportunity to fortify their case. Thus the efficacious organizing by the landfill's opponents, the willingness of the city of New Haven to undertake legal action, and the growing opposition among elected officials to landfill expansion provided an environment in 1995 that was radically transformed from the one that the Siting Authority would have encountered in 1986. By 1995, the parties to the conflict had achieved greater parity in their ability to competently present their arguments to the Siting Authority.

The mechanism created by the Indiana legislature in 1981 represented both state and local interests in the decision-making process for siting hazardous and radioactive waste facilities; the state retained a voting majority over local interests, however. When the statute creating the Siting Authority was originally passed, many assumed the law was written so that the state could overrule local opposition if the governor or elected state representatives believed there was a need for a facility that localities might reject. In the case of the Adams Center Landfill, however, then-governor Evan Bayh had expressed some sympathies for the concerns raised by the Dump Stoppers. It might be argued that he appointed people to the Siting Authority who at least were open-minded about the issues raised by residents; none, however, was ever challenged for bias by Chemical Waste Management. The statewide members exemplified the key economic constituencies in the state: business, agriculture, and labor. They were supplemented by well-respected scientific experts. The contending local jurisdictions were apportioned their own representatives, with Chemical Waste Management eventually challenging the appointments of Allen County and New Haven, but not those of the city of Fort Wayne, the entity with whom it had the strongest legal, political, and financial ties. The members of the Siting Authority fulfilled their function by listening carefully to the information presented to them at the initial eleven-hour public hearing, evaluating closely the supplemental materials submitted during the intervening period, and, finally, intently participating in the adjudicatory phase of the hearing. Chemical Waste Management may have pressed for the adjudicatory hearings because of its extensive legal and financial resources, yet, in the end, its presentation to the Siting Authority may have raised more doubts than certainty about the environmental, economic, and social benefits of the landfill. The nine individuals on the Siting Authority, given access to vast amounts of information about the likely impacts of such a facility, and taking as their mission the deciphering of the public good on this matter, decided it was not wise to let the landfill expand, that its overall costs simply outweighed its potential benefits. What had until then been a largely adversarial set of processes, focused initially on the technical issues of risk and then played out in the contentious arena of the courts, briefly left the terrain of competing interests during the Siting Authority deliberations. The Siting Authority members sought to comprehend and then to act on what they believed to be the public interest in this matter.[60] The Siting Authority may provide a useful model, therefore, for a deliberative process in the public sphere, linked to the governmental sector, that resulted in actual policy outcomes. Still, the Siting Authority may not have functioned as effectively as it did in this case had political and social factors not been present to provide a greater-than-usual balance of powers among contending interests.

POSTSCRIPT

The capping of the Adams Center Hazardous Waste Landfill in June 1998 was not the end of the conflict over the site. In March 2001, five years after the Siting Authority ruling, the opponents of the landfill's expansion met both to celebrate that victory and to announce that their focus now would be on the future uses of the landfill and the surrounding acreage, which was still owned by Chemical Waste Management. The city of New Haven still had a lawsuit pending against Chemical Waste Management and Allen County concerning violations of the 1974 restrictive land-use covenants. Landfill opponents expressed a hope that the ownership of the land surrounding the landfill would be transferred to some representative entity that would have the authority to begin planning, in an open and inclusive manner, for a sound environmental and economic future for the site. Under the Resources Conservation and Recovery Act, Chemical Waste Management was responsible for monitoring the actual landfill for thirty years after the capping. Some members of the Dump Stoppers also talked about "reparations" for the harm done and the costs borne by the local community during the years of landfill operation. However, by September of 2001, the newly elected mayor of Fort Wayne (the mayor serving at the time of the Adams Center Landfill dispute had reached his three-term limit) had formed a highly selective task force, which met behind closed doors, to delve into options for the use of the landfill and the surrounding acreage. New Haven had also elected a new mayor; the mayor involved in the organized opposition to the landfill's expansion had lost his run for a fourth term. The new mayor of New Haven agreed to participate on the Fort Wayne task force, with no consultation with the New Haven City Council; also participating on the task force were representatives from a newly formed Fort Wayne–Allen County Economic Development Alliance. The task force reviewed a proposal that involved giving

some of the land south of the landfill to the Fort Wayne Interdenominational Ministerial Alliance, a clergy group, many of whose members were
African American. The group had previously worked with Chemical
Waste Management on the city redevelopment fund created under the
annexation agreement with Fort Wayne. Another parcel of the land was
to be given to a police officer with the Fort Wayne Police Department to
run a horse farm for "at-risk" children. The major portion of the land,
east of the landfill, would be transferred to the Fort Wayne–Allen County
Economic Development Alliance.

The proposal was presented at a series of hastily assembled, poorly
attended public hearings. The agreement then came before the New
Haven City Council for its consideration. The newly elected mayor of
New Haven was chastised by the members of the council and members
of the public for the closed-door nature of the meetings with Fort Wayne
and the absence of meaningful public deliberation about the uses to
which this land, a source of great pain for so many, over so many years,
would now be put. A proposal developed by a colleague and myself, as
a result of an inquiry made by a lawyer representing the new mayor of
New Haven, with the approval of the lawyers representing the New
Haven City Council and the Dump Stoppers, was presented to the contending interests to try to break the impasse, but it was never acted upon.
The proposal called for a three-stage process to promote democratic
deliberation on the future of the landfill. The first stage would involve
interviews with the key participants in the dispute to develop a list of
options for how the landfill area should be developed. The second stage
would involve a survey sent to residents within a certain radius around
the landfill, asking them to rank the options developed based on the interviews. The third stage would involve face-to-face deliberations among the
key interests in the dispute to evaluate the public's responses to the survey. An attempt would be made to define a common interest on this matter and produce from it a policy proposal that would then have to be
ratified by elected officials in Fort Wayne and New Haven.

In June 2002, Chemical Waste Management went before the Fort Wayne
Board of Zoning Appeals to ask that the restrictive land-use covenants
created in 1974, which were the basis for New Haven's remaining lawsuit
against Chemical Waste Management, be nullified. After a contentious
public hearing, the Fort Wayne Board of Zoning Appeals decided to delay
its ruling on the request until late September 2002, perhaps hoping that
the contending parties might reach some agreement between themselves.
In the summer of 2002, Chemical Waste Management announced that it
was transferring land south of the landfill to the Fort Wayne Interdenominational Ministerial Alliance. This nongovernmental group had little
experience in economic development, and it appeared unlikely to have

the legitimacy to convene the various interests still at odds over the land-fill's future. The long-serving Fort Wayne City Council representative from the largely minority council district on the southeast side of Fort Wayne, an early supporter of and active contributor to the work of the Dump Stoppers, had died several years earlier. After his death, and with the replacement of the New Haven mayor with whom he had worked so closely, Chemical Waste Management's financial inroads into some of the institutions of the African American community in southeast Fort Wayne were strengthened, and the coalition between the Allen County Dump Stoppers and at least some minority residents of southeast Fort Wayne weakened. This then diminished the role that a strong community/environmental/public interest constituency could exert to counter the short-term economic development perspectives of local government and business interests on this matter. So, although an array of community, environmental, and public interests came together in a vibrant enough social and political coalition to force a social, economic, and environmental review of the Adams Center Hazardous Waste Landfill before the Indiana Hazardous Waste Facility Site Approval Authority, those interests have not yet developed a viable mechanism for democratically deliberating about the future uses of the landfill site.

NOTES

1. Unless otherwise indicated, the material in this chapter is based on previously published research on the Adams Center Hazardous Waste Landfill (Jane Grant, "Assessing and Managing Risk in the Public Sector: An Urban Hazardous Waste Landfill," *Journal of Urban Affairs* 16, no. 4 [1994]: 335–358) and subsequent observation of events, analysis of documents, review of newspaper articles, and interviews with key participants in the continuing landfill conflict.

2. G. Tyler Miller Jr., *Living in the Environment: Principles, Connections, and Solutions*, 12th ed. (Belmont, Calif.: Wadsworth/Thomson Learning, 2002), 519–520, 543.

3. Michael B. Gerrard, *Whose Backyard, Whose Risk: Fear and Fairness in Toxic and Nuclear Waste Siting* (Cambridge, Mass.: MIT Press, 1994), 7–24.

4. Miller, *Living in the Environment*, 518, 543–544; Gerrard, *Whose Backyard*, 7–24.

5. United States Census Bureau, *Profile of General Demographic Characteristics: 2000*, Table DP-1 (Washington, D.C.: Census Bureau, 2000).

6. John Bartlow Martin, *Indiana: An Interpretation*, with an introduction by James H. Madison (Bloomington: Indiana University Press, 1992); Robert D. Shangle and Barbara Shangle, *Discovering Indiana* (Beaverton, Oreg.: American Products, 2000).

7. Martin, *Indiana*, 8

8. U.S. Census Bureau, "Profile of Selected Economic Characteristics: 2000,

Table DP-3," Census 2000. In 2000, a little over 14 percent of the comparative U.S. civilian population were employed in manufacturing (Summary File 3).

9. U.S. Census Bureau, Table DP-3. In 2000, almost 20 percent of the comparative U.S. civilian population were employed in education, health, and social services (Summary File 3).

10. U.S. Census Bureau, Table DP-3, 2000. In 2000, a little over 16 percent of the comparative U.S. civilian population were employed in finance, insurance, real estate, professional, scientific, and waste management jobs, while retail trade accounted for almost 12 percent of employment in the general U.S. civilian population (Summary File 3).

11. U.S. Census Bureau, Table DP-3, 2000. In 2000, the median household income in the United States was $41,994 (Summary File 3).

12. U.S. Census Bureau, Table DP-1, 2000. In 2000, over 12 percent of the U.S. population were listed as African American and 12.5 percent were listed as Hispanic (Summary File 3).

13. U.S. Census Bureau, "Profile of Selected Housing Characteristics: Table DP-4, 2000." In 2000, the median home value in the United States was $119,600 and over 62 percent of the housing units were owner occupied (Summary File 3).

14. Grant, "Assessing and Managing Risk."

15. Grant, "Assessing and Managing Risk."

16. Grant, "Assessing and Managing Risk," 341.

17. Grant, "Assessing and Managing Risk."

18. Grant, "Assessing and Managing Risk."

19. Michael Edelstein, *Contaminated Communities: The Social and Psychological Impacts of Residential Toxic Exposure* (Boulder, Colo.: Westview, 1988, 7); Grant, "Assessing and Managing Risk."

20. Grant, "Assessing and Managing Risk"; Edelstein, *Contaminated Communities*, 7–8.

21. Grant, "Assessing and Managing Risk."

22. Grant, "Assessing and Managing Risk."

23. Sheldon Krimsky and Alonzo Plough, *Environmental Hazards: Communicating Risks as a Social Process* (Dover, Mass.: Auburn House, 1988), 1–12.

24. Edelstein, *Contaminated Communities*, 118–137.

25. Caron Chess, video conference participant, "Expert Review and Public Assessment of Issues Related to the Adams Center Hazardous Waste Landfill in Fort Wayne, Indiana," *Panel One: Public Process*. Taped at Indiana University–Purdue University, Fort Wayne, Indiana, 23 May 1994.

26. Edelstein, *Contaminated Communities*, 170–189.

27. Glen Hall, "Judge Erects New Hurdles to Landfill Growth," (Fort Wayne, Ind.) *Journal Gazette*, 30 August 1994, 1–2 (A).

28. Grant, "Assessing and Managing Risk," 1994.

29. City of New Haven, "Who Said Life Was Fair? The Adams Center Hazardous Waste Landfill" (Fort Wayne, Ind.: Custom Video Communications, 19 August 1993), videotape; Grant, "Assessing and Managing Risk," 1994.

30. Grant, "Assessing and Managing Risk."

31. *The City of New Haven, Indiana, v. Board of Zoning Appeals of Allen County,*

Indiana, Allen County Administrator Dennis A. Gordon, Chemical Waste Management of Indiana, Inc., Indiana Department of Environmental Management and Indiana Hazardous Waste Facility Site Approval Authority, Cause No. 02D01-9302-CP-308 in the Allen Superior Court.

32. Indiana Code 13-7-8.6. *Hazardous or Low Level Nuclear Waste Facility Site Approval Authority,* 1981.

33. Indiana Code 13-7-8.6.

34. Grant, "Assessing and Managing Risk."

35. Hall, "Judge Erects New Hurdles," 1–2 (A).

36. Glen Hall, "County Asks Halt to Landfill Growth," (Fort Wayne, Ind.) *Journal Gazette,* 31 August 1994, 1 (C).

37. Jim Chapman, "Ruling Favors Landfill Expansion," (Fort Wayne, Ind.) *Journal Gazette,* 24 November 1994, 1–2 (A).

38. Anne Marie Obiala, "Landfill Asks OK to Build East, West," (Fort Wayne, Ind.) *Journal Gazette,* 22 June 1995, 1–2 (A).

39. Indiana Code 13-7-8.6, 3.

40. Anne Marie Obiala, "Siting Authority Member Biased, Landfill Owner Says," (Fort Wayne, Ind.) *Journal Gazette,* 10 January 1996, 1–2 (C); Anne Marie Obiala, "New Haven Delegate Stays on Landfill Panel," (Fort Wayne, Ind.) *Journal Gazette,* 20 January 1996, 1–2 (A); Anne Marie Obiala, "Landfill Conflicts Alleged; New Haven Official Quits Siting Authority," (Fort Wayne, Ind.) *Journal Gazette,* 15 March 1996, 1 (C).

41. Anne Marie Obiala, "Panel Gets Earful," (Fort Wayne, Ind.) *Journal Gazette,* 21 January 1996, 1, 4 (A).

42. Anne Marie Obiala, "Pared Landfill Plan Given OK," (Fort Wayne, Ind.) *Journal Gazette,* 7 March 1996, 1, 2 (C).

43. I served as an expert witness for the city of New Haven; I presented the findings of my published research (1994) and discussed the history of decision making concerning the landfill and the consequences for social trust when public decision-making processes inadequately account for the risk perceptions of, and ineffectively involve, those likely to bear the most direct consequences of an unwanted local facility.

44. Jane Mansbridge, *Beyond Adversary Democracy* (Chicago: University of Chicago Press, 1983), 5.

45. Bob Caylor, "Chem Waste Expansion Denied," (Fort Wayne, Ind.) *News Sentinel,* 22 March 1996, 1–2 (A).

46. Caylor, "Chem Waste Expansion Denied," 1–2 (A).

47. Jim Chapman, "Landfill Saga Not Done Yet: Location Tipped Scales against Expansion Plans," (Fort Wayne, Ind.) *Journal Gazette,* 23 March 1996, 1–2 (A).

48. Anne Marie Cox, "Landfill Wins Expansion Bout," (Fort Wayne, Ind.) *Journal Gazette,* 21 October 1997, 1 (A) and 2 (A).

49. Anne Marie Obiala, "Adams Center Denied Again," (Fort Wayne, Ind.) *Journal Gazette,* 11 April 1996, 1–2 (C).

50. Indiana Hazardous Waste Facility Site Approval Authority, "Findings of Fact, Conclusions of Law and Final Order Regarding the Application for a CEC Submitted by Chemical Waste Management of Indiana, L.L.C." (Indianapolis: Indiana Hazardous Waste Facility Site Approval Authority, 7 May 1996).

51. Anne Marie Obiala, "Both Sides Approve Settlement on Landfill," (Fort Wayne, Ind.) *Journal Gazette*, 20 July 1996, 1–2 (A).

52. Anne Marie Obiala, "Landfill Seeks to Grow by 24 Acres," (Fort Wayne, Ind.) *Journal Gazette*, 7 May 1997, 1–2 (A).

53. Anne Marie Cox, "IDEM Denies Landfill Expansion," (Fort Wayne, Ind.) *Journal Gazette*, 14 June 1997, 1–2 (A).

54. Anne Marie Cox, "Landfill Wins Expansion Bout," (Fort Wayne, Ind.) *Journal Gazette*, 21 October 1997, 1–2 (A).

55. Anne Marie Cox, "Judge Reopens Landfill Bid," (Fort Wayne, Ind.) *Journal Gazette*, 5 November 1997, 1–2 (A).

56. Anne Marie Cox, "Landfill to Halt Operation: Suspension Effective in Mid-1998," (Fort Wayne, Ind.) *Journal Gazette*, 26 November 1997, 1 and 9 (A).

57. Laura Emerson, "Landfill to Be Capped after Last Load in Late May," (Fort Wayne, Ind.) *Journal Gazette*, 23 April 1998, 1, 2 (A).

58. Jeff Bailey and Joan S. Lublin, "Waste Management Stock Falls 20% as CEO Quits," *Wall Street Journal*, 31 October 1997, 3, 8 (A).

59. Douglas Amy, "Environmental Dispute Resolution: The Promise and Pitfalls," in *Environmental Policy in the 1990s,* ed. Norman J. Vig and Michael E. Kraft (Washington, D.C.: Congressional Quarterly, 1990), 211–234.

60. Robert Dahl, *Controlling Nuclear Weapons: Democracy versus Guardianship* (Syracuse: Syracuse University Press, 1985); Roger Fisher and William Ury, *Getting to Yes: Negotiating Agreement without Giving In*, ed. Bruce Patton, 2nd ed. (New York: Penguin, 1991).

4

The Environment, Energy Policy, and Sustainable Development in the United States: Historical Antecedents and Future Prospects

> We have been too self-absorbed to foresee the long-term conse-
> quences of our actions, and we will suffer a terrible loss unless we
> shake off our delusions and move quickly to a resolution. Science and
> technology led us into this bottleneck. Now science and technology
> must help us find our way through and out.
>
> —Edward O. Wilson, *The Future of Life*

While the experience of the Indiana Hazardous Waste Facility Site Approval Authority provides some insights into how a protracted environmental policy dispute might benefit from a deliberative forum that examines a variety of perspectives and focuses on issues of fairness and the common good, planning for the Adams Center Hazardous Waste Landfill was, for most of its contentious history, either nonexistent or reactive. A number of analysts have suggested[1] that the relationship of human beings to the natural environment is presently at a critical juncture, one that will require a new paradigm to reshape and reorient the culture and institutions of twenty-first-century societies toward an "ethic of sustainability."[2] This ethic centers on the responsibility of humans to recognize and more carefully plan for the impacts of human activities on natural systems. What form, what shape these planning processes might take is largely emergent, although some communities in the United States[3] and even entire nations[4] have begun to develop approaches. In the United States, instrumentalities that are most likely to be effective will be rooted in our culture, our history, and our social, political, and economic institutions. While developing out of our past, these efforts must also be suited to the rapidly changing conditions of the modern world.

One issue that has gone largely unplanned in the public arena in the United States and yet is central to any future planning for the environment is energy. Energy is to a significant degree at the heart of the contemporary environmental crisis. Although it may be an oversimplification to define energy consumption per capita as a measure of a society's development,[5] it is also clear that energy is central to the fundamental institutions of any society, and the more industrialized a society, the more that energy needs pervade it. The centrality of energy to an industrialized society is in fact one of the reasons that creating a concerted national energy policy is so difficult. Here, after all, is a policy problem that affects all sectors of a society, has a multiplicity of interests attached to its production and consumption, and, yet, whose resolution may have vast implications for the viability of life on the planet. Energy issues are tightly bound up not only with questions of resource availability but with severe pollution consequences, as well. In 1987, the United Nations World Commission on Environment and Development[6] noted that, despite the variety of beliefs, values, and organizational systems that characterize the nations of the earth, we ultimately share a common fate; the commission's hope was that by acting collaboratively to address and simultaneously plan for economic growth and environmental protection, we could begin to affirmatively shape "our common future." This chapter will examine some of the ways Americans have historically defined their relationship to the natural environment, as well as looking at the range of contemporary orientations to the environment in the United States. It will also explore some of the emergent issues in environmental and energy policies and politics in the United States, provide a brief overview of energy use in this country, and suggest some of the issues that will be central to deliberating about our energy future.

THE ENVIRONMENT IN U.S. HISTORY

The land in North America that European colonists began to settle in the early seventeenth century was populated by communities that relied on hunting and gathering for survival.[7] Although there may have been and still are significant differences among Native Americans in terms of their cultural and institutional orientations to the natural environment, hunting and gathering societies tend to have limited and largely local impacts on their environment due to small population numbers and restricted technologies. The colonists, on the other hand, began the transition to an agricultural stage of development, in which the impacts on the surrounding environment were much greater. In agricultural societies, natural cycles are subjected to increasing human controls, especially through the domestication of plants and animals and the use of new technologies. A more stable food supply allows for settled communities and increased population growth. And with the bounty of natural resources in the "new world," it was easy to believe in their limitlessness. If a particular area was shorn of its riches or subjected to unwanted degradation, plentiful new vistas beckoned. The colonists obviously had pressing problems of survival to face; in addition, they faced the challenges of becoming independent of Great Britain and creating the bases for the political, social, and economic institutions that survive today.

It is clear that among the founders, Thomas Jefferson, for one, had a vision of an enduring agrarian society, in which families living on their own small farms would be bound to communities and actively participated in their own governance. In fact, the belief in a civic republic was predicated on the autonomy that landownership afforded and the opportunities it permitted citizens to forge the conditions under which they lived. However, the emergence of an industrial society in the United States began to be obvious even by the second decade of the nineteenth century and became fully dominant soon after the Civil War.[8] It was the early signs of an industrial society's effects on the relationship of citizens to one another, on their ability to manage their lives, and on the natural environment that gave rise to a chorus of concerns about the direction in which the country was headed. Beginning in the period from about 1830 to 1870, evidence from Great Britain, as well as from the United States, prompted citizens such as Ralph Waldo Emerson, Henry David Thoreau, George Catlin, and George Perkins Marsh[9] to express alarm about a declining civic virtue, a growing emphasis on materialism, and an increased negligence in our association with the land and other natural resources. These same concerns also gave rise in America to numerous utopian and communal experiments, whose focus was to create alternatives to the grim realities of an emerging industrial capitalism.[10]

Following the Civil War, more extensively organized social and political responses and more formalized governmental initiatives concerning the environment appeared. In the decades from 1870 to 1920, activism emerged over land-use and resource-management issues, as well as pollution and urban reform issues.[11] Robert Gottlieb analyzes the radical and reformist wings of both the land management and urban pollution movements. The more radical "preservationists," such as John Muir, who founded the Sierra Club in 1892, emerged alongside of the more reform-minded "conservationists," such as Teddy Roosevelt. Muir represented an emphasis on harmonious coexistence with, thoughtful stewardship over, and restraint from exploitation of the natural environment; in the contemporary environmental movement, this orientation is labeled "eco-centric."[12] Like Henry David Thoreau, Muir and his compatriots believed in treading lightly on the land and preserving it in as much of a pristine state as possible. Conservationists like Teddy Roosevelt and his secretary of the interior, Gifford Pinchot, believed, on the other hand, that humans had a right to extract resources for their own use from nature; they had the prerogative to dominate nature, but they had a responsibility to also wisely manage it. This orientation, which today is characterized as "anthropocentric," places humans at the center of ecosystems and attaches to humans the ingenuity to profitably extract resources from the environment and cleverly manage the impacts of their removal, with few limitations.[13]

At the same time that social and political groups emerged to argue over land-use and resources management, and probably partly in response to them, the federal government of the United States created the first institutions to manage land and natural resources. They ranged from the National Forest Service, established in 1905, whose multiple-use and sustainable-yield principle echoed the conservationists' "wise use" philosophy, to the National Park Service, established in 1916, whose restrictions on use reflected the preservationists' orientation toward leaving natural places as wild as possible. The later establishment, in 1964, of national wilderness areas perhaps has come closest to the eco-centric visions of Muir and Thoreau; although they comprise only 4 percent of the land area in the United States, wilderness areas are tightly restricted, even, in some cases, for recreational uses.[14]

As groups engaged in conflicts over land use and natural resources management, a parallel set of debates was emerging over industrial pollution in urban areas.[15] The founders and supporters of Hull House in Chicago, including Jane Addams, Florence Kelley, Alice Hamilton, John Dewey, and Upton Sinclair, outlined a more radical vision to improve the conditions of the poor. These reformers were concerned about the exposure of urban dwellers to industrial toxins and waste materials in their workplaces and neighborhoods. They were also disturbed by the declining control that citizens of the new industrial age were able to exercise over their lives; they argued for fundamental changes in the organization and accountability of emerging economic, social, and political institutions.[16] The more moderate reformers pushed for bureaucratic and institutional mechanisms to control the impacts of industrialization. These included the creation of the U.S. Public Health Service in 1912 and the promulgation of national regulations regarding sanitation and water quality. In trying to set limits on industry, rather than restructure it, these advocates were regarded as less radical than those affiliated with Hull House.[17]

The progressive movement in politics also helped to institutionalize in government what it perceived as a needed counterweight to the increasing concentration and power of business in America. Teddy Roosevelt was among those arguing for the centralization and professionalization of the federal government in order to limit the influence of big business in society. Others, like Louis Brandeis, argued for the decentralization of economic institutions, dispersing concentrated power and returning control to local communities. Besides the centralizing and decentralizing efforts to deal with the influence of industry in America, a third orientation argued for increasing consumer rights. By the 1930s, this orientation became quite significant, as the nation turned increasingly away from the ideal of the civic republic (in which citizens act in concert to govern themselves) and began to focus instead on the priority of individual rights as the cornerstone of equality in the emerging procedural republic.[18]

These efforts at political, social, and environmental reform were slowed as the nation faced the ravages of the Great Depression; some analysts have argued, in fact, that the changes institutionalized under the New Deal helped to forestall the more radical demands being espoused in both urban and rural centers throughout the country.[19] Nonetheless, several programs enacted by the Roosevelt administration during the early years of FDR's presidency were significant because they continued in the civic republican tradition, while producing important environmental benefits. The Civilian Conservation Corps (CCC) put young, unemployed men to work on natural restoration projects, including the building of state parks, the replanting of trees, and the protection of wildlife. CCC members learned new and valuable skills, and since their basic needs for food and shelter were provided for by the corps, they had income to send back to their families and local communities. At the same time, corps members were engaged in important conservation efforts.[20] The Tennessee Valley Authority (TVA) also served a dual purpose; it involved local citizens in decision making, while making rural electrification projects available to sections of the country that lacked access to such power.[21] The creation of the Soil Erosion Service, later the Soil Conservation Service, while largely institutionalized through a bureaucracy, nonetheless addressed a critical environmental need at the time.[22]

The adoption of a Keynesian economic approach in the late 1930s and the entrance into World War II in 1942 provided the economic stimulus that eventually ended the Great Depression; with them came the further weakening of the civic orientation in the United States and the ascendance of a procedural ethos.[23] This meant abandoning the hope of creating institutions in which citizens might act together to respond to social problems, and replacing it with programs that provided funds for individuals to choose their own routes to a meaningful and satisfying life. (Social security and related unemployment, disability, and health care benefits programs best symbolize this trend.) With the unleashing of the industrial economy at the end of World War II, the emergence of the baby boom, and the suburbanization of the American dream, the United States became centrally focused on economic growth and the unparalleled acquisition of mass consumer goods.[24] Yet, even during this spiral of affluence—and perhaps because of it[25]—new voices appeared, akin to those a century before that decried the decline in civic virtue, the attachment to material wealth, and the loss of respect for the natural world. Critics of unrestrained consumerism, during the 1950s and the 1960s, included Paul and Percival Goodman, Herbert Marcuse, and members of the Beat Generation. They foreshadowed a period of growing criticism of the major institutions of the society during the 1960s, which included the student free speech and antiwar movements, the Civil Rights movement, the women's movement, the New Left and the counterculture, and a newly unfolding environmental movement. The contemporary environmental movement received moral inspiration from the works of Rachel Carson, particularly *Silent Spring*, published in 1962.[26] Schnaiberg[27] argued that the environmental movement of the late 1960s and the early 1970s was a genuine social movement, securely based in the American middle class. One of the weaknesses of the movement then, and some would say still, was its failure to forge meaningful alliances with the poor and the working class. The poor, although often the victims of industrial pollution in their own communities, were focused on issues of survival; the failure to link potential new economic opportunities for the poor to a sustainable development strategy marred the movement, then and now. The working class, on the other hand, were often employed in the industries that were the target of environmental concern, from timber harvesting to oil refining; feeling their livelihoods and their communities threatened by environmentalism, blue-collar workers were not likely to be strong supporters of the movement.[28]

The crowning achievement of the contemporary environmental movement was the passage of the environmental legislation that has become the cornerstone of environmental protection in the United States. The Clean Air Act, the Clean Water Act, the Endangered Species Act, and the Resources Conservation and Recovery Act, among many other critical pieces of legislation passed by the U.S. Congress in the 1960s and 1970s, institutionalized the concerns raised by environmental activists and middle-class constituencies at this time. The National Environmental Policy

Act (NEPA), passed in 1969, outlined a noble vision of environmental protection in the United States, while the Environmental Protection Agency (EPA), created in 1970, provided a bureaucratic mechanism to coordinate the variety of statutes being passed. Of course, the fact that the EPA has never achieved cabinet-level status in our government and the fact that it deals largely with pollution issues, while issues of resource management are spread among a variety of other federal departments and agencies, attest to the strong resistance this nation still has to envisioning environmental policy as an integral aspect of planning for a secure future.[29]

Gottlieb[30] argues that the environmental movement that solidified after the first national Earth Day on April 22, 1970, can be classified into three categories: (1) the old mainline organizations, (2) the newer staff-based organizations, and (3) the radical and grassroots organizations. The mainline organizations, such as the Sierra Club, the Audubon Society, and the National Wildlife Federation, having been in existence, in some cases, for over one hundred years, remained focused on natural resources management issues and relied on volunteers for organizational maintenance; these volunteers hailed from the more affluent groups in society. Over time, these organizations would of necessity begin to look more like the professionally staffed organizations—like the Natural Resources Defense Council or Friends of the Earth—that came of age in the 1960s and the 1970s. This second group of organizations had full-time staff members, many of whom were trained in the policy and environmental sciences; they pioneered the mass membership mailing lists that came to define the interest group culture of American politics in the 1970s. These groups were focused on both resource management and pollution issues. They became quite sophisticated about the intricacies of policy institutionalization that followed the passage of legislation in the 1960s and the 1970s. The last category of groups espoused more radical philosophies regarding the environment, symbolized by the antinuclear movement and Greenpeace in the 1960s and the 1970s, Earth First! in the 1980s, and the Earth Liberation Front in the 1990s and 2000s. These groups have adopted a variety of Alinsky-style confrontational tactics, ranging from civil disobedience to eco-terrorism. At the same time, grassroots organizations emerged in response to local issues, such as the siting of hazardous and nuclear waste facilities. They have used a variety of strategies to achieve their aims, from legislative, judicial, and regulatory challenges to existing statutes to civil disobedience.

In the 1970s, while new federal environmental statutes were being institutionalized, while membership in environmental organizations grew, and while support for environmental protection remained strong,[31] a backlash against environmental protection and the new legislation it had spawned was also under way. Ronald Reagan came to symbolize this backlash. While governor of California in the 1960s, Reagan signed the state's clean air statute.[32] Yet, by the 1970s, having adopted the philosophy of "supply-side" economics and the corollary commitment to remove any restraints on economic growth, he became an adamant opponent of regulation, particularly in the environmental area. He gathered around him, in preparation for his run for the presidency, a group that came to be known as the "sagebrush rebels"; they wanted to reverse the century-long federal involvement in land and resources management. This early effort at limiting government management of public lands would later reemerge under the "property rights" and county movements in the latter part of the 1980s.[33] Before Ronald Reagan was elected to the presidency, however, Richard Nixon left his own mark on environmental administration.

Nixon's election in 1968, emphasizing a return to "law and order," can be understood, at least in part, as a response by those who had grown fearful of the momentous social upheavals they witnessed in the 1960s, and who perceived threats to their stable, middle-class, largely race-segregated communities. The "silent majority" may have been suspicious of the increasing role of the federal government in responding to the social problems revealed in the decade; yet, their sense of security was also upended by the growing list of groups asking to become full participants in the nation's polity, including African Americans, Native Americans, Hispanic Americans, the poor, women, gays and lesbians, and the disabled. Martin Marty[34] has described this conflict as that between the "totalists," who dominated our national culture through the 1950s, and the "tribalists," who emerged in the 1960s. Yet this new apprehension about the dissolution of community and the values it upheld would be a lament not only of conservatives, but of liberals and progressives as well. For the groups at the center to the left of the political spectrum, it was not the increasing size of government or the enlargement of the polity that was the threat, but rather the growing influence of corporations on government, the excessive focus on materialism prompted by a pervasive capitalist culture, the perceived lack of fairness and pronounced inequalities within society, and the impacts of unending economic growth on the natural environment. The decline of "gemeinschaft" and the ascendance of "gesellschaft," while providing new opportunities to expand the polity and to increase equality in America, also undermined the basis for Americans to actively define and meaningfully participate in that polity. The task of self-governance would now, more than ever, be relegated to the private sphere. Groups at both ends, ironically, of the political spectrum—but more successfully from the conservative end, at least in the following decades—would attempt to bring values and the issue of the good back into public discourse. Thus, the Republican Party, beginning with

Nixon's election, generally has been more successful at responding to these fears of civic decline than the Democratic Party, placing blame on the growing scale of government, the attempts at "social engineering," the restrictions on free enterprise, and the loss of "family values." Democrats, on the other hand, generally following the course set out in the latter years of the Roosevelt administration, have sought to deal with societal inequities by advancing new social and economic opportunities, while paying little attention to the values and structures within which people lead their lives. They have drawn on the classical liberal tradition, in which government is neutral toward values and rights precede the good.[35]

Richard Nixon created the United States Environmental Protection Agency (EPA) by executive order in 1970. On the one hand, Nixon still needed to respond to both congressional and interest group pressures to continue the forward momentum of environmental protection; on the other hand, cognizant of the emerging conservative base that had supported him in 1968, he wanted to exert as much control over the administration of environmental policy as he could. The agency was charged with overseeing the implementation of the newly passed environmental statutes, and, as noted earlier, it focused almost entirely on establishing and enforcing pollution regulations. The EPA was not incorporated into the cabinet, nor were its responsibilities integrated with those of the agencies in charge of land and resources management. Following the fears about the corruption of government institutions unleashed by the Watergate scandal, Jimmy Carter devoted his years in the White House to helping to restore the ethical basis of government. His focus on efficient and effective government was reminiscent of the Progressive Era. Carter attempted to deal with the energy crisis at the end of the 1970s by appealing to Americans' notion of a common good and their capabilities for self-governance.[36]

Thus, while Carter attempted to invoke a set of civil ideals as the underpinning of government itself, it was Ronald Reagan who struck a chord with the nation by appealing to the communal ethos that had guided the nation from the beginning. And while this image of Americans, situated in their communities and responsive to one another's concerns, was powerful, it operated alongside the actual deconstruction of governmental initiatives intended to provide for the common welfare. Reagan, as noted earlier, was particularly focused on the villainy of environmental regulations; his advisors understood, however, that they would be unlikely, at least in the near term, even with a Republican majority in the Senate, to convince the Congress to undo the environmental legislation passed in the 1970s. They devised instead an administrative strategy to blunt environmental protection initiatives; they appointed to head key environmental and resource management agencies personnel who were hostile to the missions of the agencies, cut agency budgets, and stalled the implementation of proposed regulations.[37] And while citizens may have been drawn to Reagan's notion of a smaller and more efficient government, they were not necessarily supportive of efforts to weaken the vital legislation that had been put in place to preserve the quality of the air, land, and water. What was seen as Ronald Reagan's assault on environmental protection produced its own backlash. Membership in environmental organizations soared, while the Democrats returned as the majority in the Senate in 1986. Ronald Reagan vetoed the revisions to the Clean Water Act in 1987, but his veto was overridden by the Congress.[38]

George H. W. Bush, in his run for the presidency in 1988, called himself "the environmental president." While wanting to benefit from Reagan's general popularity, he also wanted to distinguish himself from his predecessor in the environmental arena. As president, G. H. W. Bush appointed to key environmental posts at least some personnel who had backgrounds in environmental protection. At the same time, his chief of staff, John Sununu, a strong supply-side advocate, generally prevailed with the president in policy battles that pitted environmental protection against economic growth. Bush, like Reagan before him, also established a council, headed by his vice president, to review "unnecessary regulation." G. H. W. Bush did preside over the 1990 passage of the long-stalled Clean Air Act Amendments, which recognized the key role of sulfur and nitrogen dioxides in the production of acid rain and used the notion of tradable pollution permits as a means to curb these emissions. Still, G. H. W. Bush claimed there was not enough information to act on global climate change (as Reagan had argued with acid rain); he would not permit his representatives to the United Nations Conference on Environment and Development in Rio de Janeiro in 1992 to sign the Convention on Global Climate Change, unless mandated targets were removed. The United States did not sign the Convention on Biodiversity produced at the conference, until Bill Clinton became president.[39]

The Clinton-Gore administration should have been, on the face of it, the most environmentally oriented since the height of the modern environmental movement in the late 1960s and through the decade of the 1970s. Al Gore, author of *Earth in the Balance: Ecology and the Human Spirit* (1992), was one of the most knowledgeable members of the U.S. Congress on contemporary ecological issues. Yet the Clinton presidency was focused almost entirely on the issue of economic growth. Of course, Clinton and Gore rebuffed the strong attempts by the "Gingrich Congress" to reinvigorate the environmental deregulation movement that had begun under Ronald Reagan. And by its second term, the Clinton-Gore administration had succeeded in providing new protections for public lands and endangered species, particularly in the western United States.[40] By and large, however, the dynamic of what Schnaiberg[41] has called "managed scarcity" prevailed. In this dynamic, some limits are placed on industrial production, but, in general, it is "business as usual." What does change in these different eras is how high or low regulation standards are set.[42] Environmental protection was not any more integrated into economic planning at the end of the Clinton-Gore administration than before, although Clinton, but especially Gore, did at least argue that environmental protection could be compatible with economic growth; Gore embraced the concept of sustainable development as the path upon which the future needed to be guided.

THE ENVIRONMENT, ENERGY POLICY, AND THE GEORGE W. BUSH ADMINISTRATION

Even with the limited environmental achievements of Clinton and Gore, environmentalists may look back wistfully on those years. Although the environment was not absent from Al Gore's platform in the 2000 campaign, it was not a prominent theme of his public appearances, either. Despite his winning the popular vote, Gore's loss in the electoral college was particularly vexing because of the votes he lost to Green Party candidate Ralph Nader (particularly in Florida, of course).[43] George W. Bush's presidency, in many ways, has echoed that of Ronald Reagan's in the area of environmental policy. Within a few months of his inauguration, George W. Bush announced his administration's decision to withdraw from the Kyoto Protocol on global warming, despite a campaign promise to lower carbon dioxide emissions in the United States.[44] This caused great consternation among European leaders; besides being the world's greatest single emitter of carbon dioxide, the U.S. was needed for the treaty to reach the 55 percent of polluting signatories for implementation.[45] Mirroring Ronald Reagan's stance on the control of acid rain in the 1980s, Bush argued that more research was needed to prove whether global warming was even occurring and, if it were, whether human actions were the cause of it. In addition, Bush, like Reagan, emphasized the economic hindrances that regulatory schemes provoke; he contended that participating in the Kyoto Protocol would damage the nation's fossil fuel–driven economy.[46] Like Reagan, Bush was also comfortable in appointing to regulatory positions the leaders of the industries to be regulated; for Bush, this was particularly the case for energy policy.[47] In fact, a huge public policy debate was unleashed as a result of the Bush administration's refusal to release the names of the participants of the 2001 energy task force headed by Vice President Cheney. The General

Accounting Office, as well as two public interest groups (one a conservative group called Judicial Watch and the other a coalition of environmental organizations), sued to have the names and the nature of the
discussions revealed. In developing the energy policy of the Bush administration, Secretary of Energy Spencer Abraham "heard from more than
100 energy industry executives, trade association leaders and
lobbyists. . . . Mr Abraham did not meet with any representatives of environmental organizations or consumer groups."[48] In addition, "of the top
25 energy industry donors to the Republican Party before the November
2000 election, 18 corporations sent executives or representatives to meet
with Mr. Cheney, the [energy] task force chairman, or members of the
task force and its staff. The companies include the Enron Corporation, the
Southern Company, the Exelon Corporation, BP, the TXU Corporation,
FirstEnergy, and Anadarko Petroleum."[49] A proposal by the American
Petroleum Institute, submitted to the energy task force in March 2001,
called for an energy impact assessment of any federal agency actions; in
May 2001, President Bush issued an executive order stating that "agencies
shall prepare and submit a statement of energy effects to the administrator of the Office of Information and Regulatory Affairs, Office of Management and Budget, for those matters identified as significant energy
actions."[50]

The Bush administration energy plan was released in May 2001.[51] It
proposed relying primarily on what Amory Lovins and others have called
the "hard path" approach to solving the nation's energy crisis.[52] This
strategy focuses on finding new sources of nonrenewable fossil fuels,
such as oil, coal, and natural gas, and utilizing coal and nuclear energy to
produce centrally supplied electricity.[53] In fact, Bush's energy proposal
called for the creation of "a national electricity grid."[54] In contrast, the
"soft path approach" relies significantly on energy conservation and efficiency, while phasing out the use of nuclear power, decreasing dependence on fossil fuels, and increasing the use of a mix of renewable direct
and indirect solar energy sources.[55] Although Bush's plan also called for
some limited investments in conservation and efficiency, it overwhelm-
ingly focused on the need to increase the supply of energy in the United
States. The plan noted that "America in the year 2001 faces the most serious energy shortage since the oil embargoes of the 1970's. Without action,
projected energy shortfalls in coming years 'will inevitably undermine
our economy, our standard of living and our national security.'"[56] Jimmy
Carter, whose own administration also grappled with creating a long-
term energy policy, quickly responded to President Bush's plan by stating, "World supplies are adequate and reasonably stable, price fluctuations are cyclical, reserves are plentiful. . . . [E]xaggerating claims seem
designed to promote some long-frustrated ambitions of the oil industry

at the expense of environmental quality."[57] In addition, shortly before George W. Bush was inaugurated, a report produced by five national laboratories after three years of research concluded that, with the proper government incentives to increase energy conservation and improve energy efficiency in homes, businesses, new appliances, and power plants, the growth in demand for electricity in the United States could be decreased by 20 to 47 percent. This could eliminate the need to construct two hundred to six hundred new power plants; the Bush administration energy plan said thirteen hundred new plants would be needed in the future.[58]

The Bush administration approach to developing a national energy policy, like the Clinton administration approach to developing a national health care policy under the leadership of First Lady Hillary Clinton, symbolizes an opportunity lost to address a significant public policy problem, replete with many competing interests, from the perspective of the common good. Rather than encouraging the development of structures and forums that would permit full discussion and open-ended deliberation of policy options, in which various positions could be examined and in which underlying goals and values could be clarified, the Bush administration's energy policy task force (and the Clinton administration's health policy task force) *began* with its policy conclusions. Such an approach is flawed for two basic reasons: it risks failing to reach the best policy outcome, based on the most complete information available and the fullest scrutiny of ideas in a public setting, and it risks being seen as not legitimate, especially by those not included in the policy discussions. President Bush, of course, is not alone among recent presidents (with the exception of Jimmy Carter) who failed to provide leadership for a serious examination of energy issues and the environment in the United States. Nonetheless, the American people have consistently expressed strong support for environmental laws and the spending needed to protect the environment.[59] A Gallup poll in April 2001 found that 57 percent of Americans believed "environmental protection should be given priority, 'even at the risk of curbing economic growth.'"[60] A *New York Times/ CBS News* poll after the November 2002 midterm elections found that "by a ratio of two to one, Americans . . . thought that protecting the environment was more important than producing energy." In addition, "55 percent of respondents . . . disapproved of the White House effort to drill for oil in the Arctic National Wildlife Refuge, compared to 39 percent who approved."[61] Yet, Americans' opinions on environmental matters have always suffered from the fact that although citizens express interest in environmental protection, environmental issues are not always "salient" to them.[62] When asked about the most important issues facing the nation, and without a particular environmental problem dominating the headlines, Americans don't readily mention environmental concerns. Add to this the technical and social complexity of understanding the causes of and possible responses to most environmental problems, and it becomes more understandable that there is often a "political disconnect" between what Americans believe about the environment and how closely they hold their elected officials to account.[63]

While a majority of Americans in late 2002 disapproved of President Bush's handling of environmental matters, his personal approval ratings remained high.[64] Of course, these ratings were probably related to the salience that Americans viewed foreign policy and national security issues as having at the time. Energy policy may not appear salient to most Americans precisely because it is so complicated, because the current energy approach is producing cheap and available sources of energy, and because the dangers of the current energy strategy may not be obvious for several decades. For all of these reasons, then, it becomes ever more imperative for Americans to learn as much as they can about energy issues, to have the opportunity to discuss and deliberate about future policy directions in the openness of the public sphere, and to begin to prioritize their goals and values on energy and the environment in the United States. What form these discussions might take, what types of participation opportunities would exist, and what type of deliberative venues may be created are discussed more fully in the next chapter. Here it is important to review at least briefly the primary energy policy orientations that have characterized the nation's history up until the present.

ENERGY IN U.S. HISTORY

Like other preindustrialized societies, the United States at its founding relied on renewable sources of energy.[65] Renewable energy sources are theoretically perpetual if they are managed properly. The ultimate renewable source of energy for the earth is the sun; about "99% of the energy used to heat the earth and all of our buildings comes directly from the sun."[66] In addition, the sun provides indirect forms of renewable energy through the uneven heating of the earth and the production of air currents and wind power; through the precipitation, transpiration, and evaporation of water, resulting in the hydrologic, or water, cycle; and through the creation of biomass from photosynthesis. While the sun's direct energy is expected to last billions of years through the process of nuclear fusion, the continued use of wind, water, and biomass as energy sources depends on their proper conservation; air, water and land resources can be overused or so polluted that they are no longer renewable.[67] Thus, in addition to human and animal energies, cities and towns in early America relied on wind, water, and wood for homes and businesses.[68] It wasn't until the advent of the industrial revolution, whose impact was felt in the United States in the mid-nineteenth century, that fossil fuels became a significant part of American life. "In 1840 water wheels provided far more energy than steam engines, and wood supplied much more heat than coal. In absolute terms, steam first began to provide the majority of American manufacturing power around 1875. As late as 1915 most farm work was still performed by muscle, and at that time only one home in ten had electricity or a telephone."[69]

The transition to nonrenewable fossil fuels in the United States began with the use of coal. Fossil fuels are also indirectly the result of the sun's energy; they are the fossilized organic remains of plants and animals that have decayed under pressure in the earth's crust. Geologists believe that the conditions under which these fuels were created are unlikely to appear again in the foreseeable future; as a result, the fossil fuels found in the earth's crust, such as coal, oil, and natural gas, are finite.[70] While coal was significant in the late nineteenth and early twentieth centuries in America, its dominance was already being rivaled by oil in the second decade of the twentieth century. Oil and natural gas are found together in the earth, and in the early years of oil's use, natural gas was siphoned off as a nuisance in oil extraction. By 1950, oil and natural gas were the key components of America's energy palette.[71] Also in the 1950s, following the use of a nuclear fission bomb against Japan in World War II, the United States began its quest to create a viable commercial use for nuclear energy.[72] Although projected to provide 21 percent of the world's commercial energy and almost all of its electricity by the year 2000, nuclear power provided only 6 percent of the world's overall energy and 16 percent of its electricity in 2001. In that same year, nuclear energy provided about 20 percent of the electricity and 8 percent of the overall energy used in the United States.[73] In the beginning of the twenty-first century, 92 percent of the energy consumed in the United States came from nonrenewable sources: 39 percent from oil, 23 percent from natural gas, 22 percent from coal, and 8 percent from nuclear power.[74] The remaining 8 percent of energy in the United States was derived from renewable sources: about 4 percent from hydropower, geothermal, solar, and wind sources and about 4 percent from biomass.[75] In 2001, the percentage of energy generated from renewable sources in the United States dropped to 6 percent.[76]

There are certain advantages to using the nonrenewable fossil fuels upon which our society has grown so dependent. Conventional oil, for instance, is still relatively inexpensive, it is easily transportable, and it has a high net energy yield. However, oil, like natural gas and coal, has two major disadvantages. First, there is a finite amount of it on the earth. Identified global oil reserves (which are those that are known and economically profitable to extract) are expected to last somewhere between forty and ninety years, depending on how prudently we use this resource. Thus, many experts believe that we will need to find a substitute for oil within fifty years. And even if oil were infinite, its use creates serious pollution consequences for the earth, including the release of carbon dioxide, a major component of greenhouse gases, and nitrogen oxides, a major component of acid precipitation. Drilling for oil also causes serious land disruption and the potential to pollute soil and water. The ocean transportation of oil also has had profound environmental consequences for a variety of aquatic species, as evidenced from the Exxon Valdez Oil Spill in Prince William Sound in 1989 and the oil spilled along the Galicia coast of Spain in late 2002.[77]

Like oil, natural gas has a high net energy yield and is easily transported; however, it also suffers from the twin problems of being finite and producing significant air pollution. Still, natural gas produces less carbon dioxide per unit of energy used than either coal or oil, and known reserves of natural gas are predicted to last 125 years globally and for sixty-five to eighty years in the United States. And unlike oil, over half of which the United States imports, about 90 percent of the natural gas used in the United States is domestically produced. As a result of both its availability and its smaller role in greenhouse emissions, some have argued that natural gas ought to serve as a transition fuel for the United States, as the country charts a new energy future for the twenty-first century.[78] Finally, coal is the most abundant of the fossil fuels on earth, but it also has the most problems associated with its production and use. Identified global reserves of coal may last as long as 225 years at current usage rates (but would decline significantly if coal became a more important source of fuel in the United States or the world). At the beginning of the twenty-first century, coal provided 21 percent of the world's overall commercial energy (22 percent in the United States, as well) and 62 percent of the world's electricity (52 percent in the United States).[79] However, mining coal underground is dangerous and has resulted in significant incidences of death, injury, and lung disease in the United States and elsewhere; aboveground or strip mining of coal has considerable environmental impacts, including leaving behind highly degraded land, producing acid runoff that can contaminate nearby waterways, and releasing toxic air emissions. Coal produces more carbon dioxide per unit of energy than any other fossil fuel, and its combustion also releases carbon monoxides, sulfur dioxide, and nitrogen dioxide.[80]

Nuclear energy held, at least for some, the promise of unending clean energy when its commercial applications were being developed in the late 1940s and early 1950s. Nuclear energy's chief advantage compared with the nonrenewable fossil fuels is that it emits one-sixth of the carbon dioxide per unit of energy of coal.[81] And theoretically, with the use of breeder nuclear fission reactors, the waste products at the end of energy production are available to be used for future fissioning. However, the United States, at least, has suspended development of breeder nuclear reactors because of both the danger of the waste fuel being used in nuclear weapons and the cost of building, maintaining, and operating breeder reactors. Thus, although there is presently an ample supply of uranium, it is still a finite resource; the mining of uranium also produces human and ecosystem impacts. The 435 commercial nuclear reactors in the world, including the 103 licensed commercial plants in the United States, have four major disadvantages associated with their use. First is the catastrophic possibility of a core meltdown or an explosion of the containment building in which the reactor is located. The United States experienced a core meltdown at the Three Mile Island Nuclear Power Plant in Pennsylvania in 1979, when 50 percent of the core became molten. In addition, a release of radioactive materials into the surrounding community, although argued at the time to have no effect, has left an unexplained higher incidence of cancers downwind of the reactor, as compared with upwind.[82] The Chernobyl reactor in the Ukraine experienced both a core meltdown and an explosion of the containment building; this caused radiation to be released and spread not only over the former Soviet Union itself, but over parts of Europe, as well. The Ukrainian Health Ministry estimated the death toll from the accident to be 3,576; groups such as Greenpeace Ukraine have put the death toll at thirty-two thousand. It has been estimated that over half a million people were exposed to dangerous levels of radioactivity as a result of the accident.[83] Despite the low probability of nuclear accidents such as these, the catastrophic nature of such events when they occur and the dreadedness of their impacts make the public particularly leery about living near nuclear facilities. No new nuclear power plants have been ordered in the United States since 1978.[84]

A second major problem with nuclear power is what to do with the highly radioactive spent nuclear fuel. Such fuel, if it is reprocessed, still needs to be stored safely for ten thousand years; if it is not reprocessed, it must be stored safely for 240,000 years. Given that Americans find a fifty-year planning framework daunting, the potential schedule for this type of proposal seems unimaginable. Although the United States passed the Nuclear Waste Policy Act of 1982, no permanent repository for commercial nuclear wastes in the United States has yet been constructed. However, in 2002, both the Congress and President Bush approved the creation of such a repository at Yucca Mountain in Nevada.[85] Wastes are still being temporarily stored in deep pools of water outside of nuclear power plants in the United States, while the conflict over siting a facility at Yucca Mountain continues. Added to this problem is the fact that nuclear plants themselves become highly radioactive after thirty to forty years of use, and thus the plants themselves have to be decommissioned. Finally, nuclear energy is an expensive way to produce electricity; it has the lowest net energy yield for home space heating of all energy sources (except if an electric heat pump is used; then it is the fourth least efficient approach out of fifteen).[86]

The alternative to relying on nonrenewable fossil fuels or nuclear energy is a renewable energy strategy. Soft path advocates, such as Amory Lovins, have proposed reducing our reliance on nonrenewable fossil fuels, such as oil, natural gas, and coal; phasing out the use of nuclear power; increasing our use of direct and indirect solar energy options; and maintaining an unblinking focus on energy conservation and energy efficiency. A commitment to energy conservation and efficiency can extend the life of existing fossil fuels, produce fewer emissions, and create time to move in a thoughtful manner to a new energy approach.[87]

Experts have estimated that about 43 percent of the energy used in the United States is wasted because we have not created the devices that would more efficiently extract the potential energy available in the fuels we use. This occurs especially through inefficient electric motors, lighting systems, and motor vehicles. While fuel efficiency for American autos increased 37 percent between 1973 and 1985 to 25.9 miles per gallon, it fell to 24.5 miles per gallon in 2001.[88] In 2003, the average fuel economy for all vehicles in the United States is projected to be 23.6 miles per gallon.[89] Great energy savings would also result from improving the way we heat, cool, and light our homes and buildings. Of course, conserving energy by not using it at all, such as turning off lights in buildings that are not being used, and walking or biking instead of driving, may be among the most important energy changes we could make. The latter efforts would be made easier to implement to the extent that we better planned for commercial and residential functions in an area, so that long commutes might not be necessary.[90]

The sun's energy can be used directly through passive and active solar systems to heat and cool homes and businesses and to produce electricity. Some parts of the United States are ideal for the use of solar energy; such energy is available from 80 to 90 percent of the time in the South and West. A good portion of the central United States has solar energy available over 70 percent of the time. Even the northern sections of the United States have solar energy available 60 to 69 percent of the time, which is considered satisfactory for solar energy to provide at least some part of residential energy needs.[91] The most efficient homes would be ones designed to take advantage of the sun's energy through their architecture. South- and west-facing windows can effectively utilize the sun's energy in winter, while window overhangs and deciduous trees can block the sun's rays in summer.[92] The use of discarded tires as a building material, as pioneered by Michael Reynolds in his "Earthship" homes, allows excess sunlight to be absorbed in the summer for cooling purposes and released in the winter for heating.[93] Such passively designed solar systems, while in some cases requiring more investment initially in the building of the structure, can, with the proper use of insulating materials and energy-efficient windows, provide a significant amount of a home's heating and cooling needs. Active solar systems make use of rooftop collectors to absorb the sun's energy, using some of it directly and storing some of it in insulated tanks. Photovoltaic cells, in which a silicon wafer is used to produce an electric current directly from the sun's energy, are now considered a critical component of a renewable energy strategy; it is projected that these cells could provide 17 percent of the world's electricity by the year 2020.[94]

Indirect forms of solar energy, such as water and wind, are critical as renewable sources of electricity production. Water currently provides about 20 percent of the world's electricity (about 10 percent in the United States). The construction of dams has several negative environmental consequences, however, including the flooding of productive land, the interruption of fish migrations, and the decreased flow of silt to land below the dams. Energy experts have recommended the building of smaller, more energy-efficient dams and improving the energy efficiency of the larger dams, especially those constructed in the United States in the 1930s and 1940s. Wind is considered to have significant potential as an energy source. In the United States alone, the vast wind resources of Texas, South Dakota, and North Dakota are projected to be able to provide all of the nation's electricity needs.[95] California already derives 1.5 percent of its electricity from wind, while Denmark produces 18 percent of its electricity from wind. As a result of its commitment to the Kyoto Protocol, the European Union plans to produce 22 percent of its electricity and 12 percent of its overall energy from renewable resources by 2010.[96]

Biomass is another indirect use of the sun's energy; the use of wood and manure provides 30 percent of the energy used in developing countries for heating and cooking. The air pollutants that result from the combustion of wood and the potentially irreversible destruction of the world's forests are disadvantages to using wood in this manner. However, if the plant materials are harvested and burned sustainably, and they are grown on lands that would not be used for food crops, biomass may have some role to play in a renewable energy strategy. Some energy analysts have suggested that a key to a renewable energy future may be found in the "solar-hydrogen" revolution. Hydrogen gas may be a critical asset to a new energy strategy; when burned, the waste produced is water. Since hydrogen is not easily obtainable in the atmosphere, an electric current run through water can be an important source of hydrogen. Miller[97] and others have argued, however, that unless the electricity used to extract hydrogen from water is produced from a renewable source, the net benefits of such an energy option would be greatly minimized. The hope for a fuel cell to power automobiles is based on a similar goal of using hydrogen and water to produce an electric current; the current would run an electric motor in the "internal noncombustion engine" autos of the future, whose end product would also be water.

Determining the components that should comprise the nation's future energy goals is indeed a complex task. There are compelling reasons, however, for the public to be a part of the process, no matter the difficulties. Our energy future has crucial implications for the ethical questions raised in chapter 2: the health and well-being of those humans presently on the planet, future generations, and other species. Our energy policies also have implications for the remaining ethical issue raised in that chapter: our ability to work cooperatively on such issues with other people and other societies. Even if fossil fuels were infinite, the pollution problems they create would eventually require limits on their use. Our inability as a nation to face these consequences has led to our present unwillingness to join with other nations attempting to deal with global climate change. Opportunities for public discussion, participation, and deliberation on energy issues might not only help to provide the support needed to fully embrace global negotiations on climate change; they might also provide the willingness to implement the changed policies that would result.

NOTES

1. G. Tyler Miller, *Living in the Environment: Principles, Connections, and Solutions,* 12th ed. (Belmont, Calif.: Wadsworth Group, 2002); Edward O. Wilson, *The Future of Life* (New York: Alfred A. Knopf, 2002); Lynton K. Caldwell, *International Environmental Policy,* 3rd ed. (Chapel Hill, N.C.: Duke University Press, 1996); Jane Goodall and Marc Bekoff, *The Ten Trusts: What We Must Do for the Animals We Love* (San Francisco: HarperSanFrancisco, 2002).

2. Ted Bernard and Jora Young, *The Ecology of Hope: Communities Collaborate for Sustainability* (Gabriola Island, British Columbia: New Society, 1997), 8; The World Commission on Environment and Development, *Our Common Future* (New York: Oxford University Press, 1987).

3. Bernard and Young, *The Ecology of Hope;* William A. Shutkin, *The Land That Could Be: Environmentalism and Democracy in the Twenty-First Century* (Cambridge, Mass.: MIT Press, 2001).

4. See Gary C. Bryner, *Gaia's Wager: Environmental Movements and the Challenge of Sustainability* (Lanham, Md.: Rowman & Littlefield, 2001).

5. See David E. Nye, *Consuming Power: A Social History of American Energies* (Cambridge, Mass.: MIT Press, 1998), 1–14.

6. The World Commission, *Our Common Future*.

7. Benjamin Kline, *First along the River: A Brief History of the American Environmental Movement* (San Francisco: Acada, 1997); Miller, *Living in the Environment*, 12th ed., 23–42.

8. Michael J. Sandel, *Democracy's Discontent: America in Search of a Public Philosophy* (Cambridge, Mass.: Belknap Press of Harvard University Press, 1996), 123–200.

9. James McGregor Burns, *The Vineyard of Liberty* (New York: Vintage, 1983); Miller, *Living in the Environment*, 12th ed., 23–42; Kline, *First along the River*.

10. James McGregor Burns, *The Workshop of Democracy* (New York: Vintage, 1986); Ron E. Roberts, *The New Communes: Coming Together in America* (Englewood Cliffs, N.J.: Prentice Hall, 1971).

11. Robert Gottlieb, *Forcing the Spring: The Transformation of the American Environmental Movement* (Washington, D.C.: Island, 1993), 15–80; Miller, *Living in the Environment*, 12th ed., 23–42; Kline, *First along the River*.

12. Ben A. Minteer and Bob Pepperman Taylor, eds., *Democracy and the Claims of Nature: Critical Perspectives for a New Century* (Lanham, Md.: Rowman & Littlefield, 2002); Miller, *Living in the Environment*, 12th ed., 23–42, 740–758.

13. Miller, *Living in the Environment*, 12th ed., 23–42, 740–758.

14. Miller, *Living in the Environment*, 12th ed., 23–42.

15. Gottlieb, *Forcing the Spring*, 47–80.

16. Robert B. Westbrook, *John Dewey and American Democracy* (Ithaca, N.Y.: Cornell University Press, 1991), 13–116.

17. Gottlieb, *Forcing the Spring*, 47–80.

18. Sandel, *Democracy's Discontent*, 201–249.

19. Frances Fox Piven and Richard A. Cloward, *Poor Peoples' Movements: Why They Succeed, How They Fail* (New York: Vintage, 1979).

20. Fred E. Leake and Ray S. Carter, *Roosevelt's Tree Army: A Brief History of the Civilian Conservation Corps*, 6th ed. (St. Louis, Mo.: National Association of Civilian Conservation Corps Alumni, 1987); Miller, *Living in the Environment*, 12th ed., 23–42.

21. Miller, *Living in the Environment*, 12th ed., 23–42; Philip Selznick, *TVA and the Grassroots* (Berkeley: University of California Press, 1953). Selznick also analyzes how the TVA functioned as a "co-optative" mechanism, whereby local citizens, not fully knowledgeable about or skilled in rural electrification, easily came under the sway of the experts and political leaders who controlled the authority. Here again is a lesson about the conditions that will permit participatory and deliberative mechanisms to be truly democratic, and not empty gestures.

22. Miller, *Living in the Environment*, 12th ed., 23–42.

23. Sandel, *Democracy's Discontent*, 250–273.

24. Allan Schnaiberg, *The Environment: From Surplus to Scarcity* (New York: Oxford University Press, 1980), 150–204.

25. Allan Schnaiberg, *The Environment*, 362–411; Herbert Marcuse, *One Dimensional Man: Studies in the Ideology of Advanced Industrial Society* (Boston: Beacon, 1966).

26. Gottlieb, *Forcing the Spring*, 81–116; Miller, *Living in the Environment*, 12th ed., 23–42.

27. Schnaiberg, *Environment*, 362–411.

28. Gottlieb, *Forcing the Spring*, 235–307.

29. Michael E. Kraft and Norman J. Vig, "Environmental Policy from the 1970s to the Twenty-First Century," in *Environmental Policy*, 5th ed., ed. Norman J. Vig and Michael E. Kraft (Washington, D.C.: Congressional Quarterly, 2003), 1–32; Miller, *Living in the Environment*, 12th ed., 23–42; The World Commission, *Our Common Future*, 308–347; Gottlieb, *Forcing the Spring*, 117–161.

30. Gottlieb, *Forcing the Spring*, 117–206.

31. Michael E. Kraft and Norman Vig, "Environmental Policy from the 1970s to 2000: An Overview," in *Environmental Policy*, 4th ed., ed. Norman J. Vig and Michael E. Kraft (Washington, D.C.: CQ Press, 2000), 1–31.

32. Norman J. Vig and Michael E. Kraft, eds., *Environmental Policy in the 1980s: Reagan's New Agenda* (Washington, D.C.: Congressional Quarterly, 1984).

33. Miller, *Living in the Environment*, 12th ed., 585–628.

34. Martin Marty, *The One and the Many: America's Struggle for the Common Good* (Cambridge, Mass.: Harvard University Press, 1997).

35. Sandel, *Democracy's Discontent*, 3–54.

36. Sandel, *Democracy's Discontent*, 304–308.

37. Norman J. Vig, "Presidential Leadership and the Environment: From Reagan to Bush to Clinton," in *Environmental Policy in the 1990s*, 3rd ed., ed. Norman J. Vig and Michael E. Kraft (Washington, D.C.: CQ Press, 1997), 98–120.

38. Michael E. Kraft, "Environmental Policy in Congress: From Consensus to Gridlock," in *Environmental Policy*, 4th ed., ed. Vig and Kraft, 121–145.

39. Vig, "Presidential Leadership," 98–120.

40. Kraft and Vig, "Environmental Policy from the 1970s to 2000," 1–31; Vig, "Presidential Leadership," 98–120.

41. Schnaiberg, *Environment*, 425.

42. Allan Schnaiberg and Kenneth Alan Gould, *Environment and Society: The Enduring Conflict* (New York: St. Martin's, 1994), 45–67.

43. Christopher J. Bosso and Deborah Lynn Guber, "The Boundaries and Contours of American Environmental Activism," in *Environmental Policy*, 5th ed., ed. Vig and Kraft, 79–102.

44. Douglas Jehl, "Bush Ties Policy Shift to an 'Energy Crisis,' " *New York Times*, 15 March 2001, 19 (A); Douglas Jehl, "U.S. Going Empty-Handed to Meeting on Global Warming," *New York Times*, 29 March 2001, 22 (A).

45. Edmund L. Andrews, "Bush Angers Europe by Eroding Pact on Warming," *New York Times*, 1 April 2001, 3 (1).

46. Peter S. Wenz, "Justice, Democracy, and Global Warming," *Democracy and the Claims of Nature*, ed. Minteer and Taylor, 191–214.

47. Katherine Q. Seelye, "Bush Picks Industry Leaders to Fill Environmental Posts," *New York Times*, 12 May 2001, 1, 12 (A); Don Van Natta Jr. and Neela Baner-

jee, "Bush Policies Have Been Good to Energy Industry," *New York Times*, 21 April 2002, 22 (1).

48. Don Van Natta Jr. and Neela Banerjee, "Top GOP Donors in Energy Industry Met Cheney Panel," *New York Times*, 1 March 2002, 1, 15 (A); Don Van Natta Jr. and Neela Banerjee, "Documents Show Energy Official Met Only with Industry Leaders," *New York Times*, 27 March 2002, 1, 20 (A).

49. Van Natta and Banerjee, "Bush Policies."

50. Don Van Natta Jr. and Neela Banerjee, "Review Shows Energy Industry's Recommendations to Bush Ended up Being National Policy," *New York Times*, 28 March 2002, 16 (A).

51. Douglas Jehl, "Bush, Pushing Energy Plan, Offers Scores of Proposals to Find New Power Sources," *New York Times*, 18 May 2001, 1, 14 (A).

52. Dorothy Zinberg, ed., *Uncertain Power: The Struggle for a National Energy Policy* (New York: Pergamon, 1983), xxvi.

53. Amory B. Lovins, "Technology Is the Answer (but What Was the Question?)," in Miller, *Living in the Environment*, 12th ed., 361–362.

54. Douglas Jehl, "Bush, Pushing Energy Plan."

55. Miller, *Living in the Environment*, 12th ed., 358–394.

56. David E. Sanger, "In Energy Plan, Bush Urges New Drilling, Conservation and Nuclear Power Review," *New York Times*, 17 May 2001, 1, 16 (A).

57. David E. Sanger and Joseph Kahn, "Battle Lies Ahead: Critics Say Clean Energy and Conservation Are Given Short Shrift," *New York Times*, 18 May 2001, 1, 14 (A).

58. Joseph Kahn, "Federal Reports at Odds with a Bush Plan," *New York Times*, 6 May 2001, 1, 22 (A).

59. Robert Cameron Mitchell, "Public Opinion and the Green Lobby: Poised for the 1990s," in *Environmental Policy*, 3rd ed., ed. Vig and Kraft, 81–102.

60. Bosso and Guber, "Boundaries and Contours," 81.

61. Adam Nagourney and Janet Elder, "Positive Rating for the G.O.P., If Not Its Policy," *New York Times*, 26 November 2002, 1, 22 (A).

62. Mitchell, "Public Opinion."

63. Bosso and Guber, "Boundaries and Contours."

64. Nagourney and Elder, "Positive Rating."

65. Nye, *Consuming Power*, 1–42.

66. Miller, *Living in the Environment*, 12th ed., 332.

67. Miller, *Living in the Environment*, 12th ed., 2–23, 358–394.

68. Nye, *Consuming Power*, 1–42.

69. Nye, *Consuming Power*, 6.

70. Miller, *Living in the Environment*, 12th ed., 320–357.

71. Nye, *Consuming Power*, 187–215.

72. Kai Erikson, *A New Species of Trouble: Explorations in Disaster, Trauma, and Community* (New York: Norton, 1994), 185–225.

73. G. Tyler Miller, *Living in the Environment: Principles, Connections, and Solutions*, 13th ed. (Belmont, Calif.: Wadsworth Group, 2004), 366–367.

74. Miller, *Living in the Environment*, 13th ed., 351. Although nuclear power is not derived from a fossil fuel, it is dependent on the mining of uranium, a nonre-

newable mineral found in the earth's crust. See Miller, *Living in the Environment*, 13th ed., 367.

75. Miller, *Living in the Environment*, 13th ed., 351.

76. Matthew L. Wald, "Use of Renewable Energy Took a Big Fall in 2001," *New York Times*, 8 December 2002, 40 (1).

77. Miller, *Living in the Environment*, 12th ed., 320–357; Emma Daly, "Aquarium in Spain Faces Disaster with Oil Spilled from Ship at Its Walls," *New York Times*, 24 November 2002, 12 (1).

78. Miller, *Living in the Environment*, 12th ed., 320–357.

79. Miller, *Living in the Environment*, 13th ed., 351, 363.

80. Miller, *Living in the Environment*, 12th ed., 320–357.

81. Miller, *Living in the Environment*, 12th ed., 320–357.

82. Kim A. McDonald, "Increased Cancers Tied to Nuclear Accident," *Chronicle of Higher Education*, 14 March 1997, 16 (A); Miller, *Living in the Environment*, 12th ed., 320–357.

83. Miller, *Living in the Environment*, 12th ed., 350.

84. Sheldon Krimsky and Alonzo Plough, *Environmental Hazards: Communicating Risks as a Social Process* (Dover, Mass.: Auburn, 1988), 1–12; Miller, *Living in the Environment*, 12th ed., 347.

85. Alison Mitchell, "Senate Approves Nuclear Waste Site in Nevada Mountain," *New York Times*, 10 July 2002, 14 (A). A repository was opened in Carlsbad, New Mexico, in 1999 for the spent wastes of nuclear weapons production in the United States; see James Brooke, "Deep Desert Grave Awaits First Load of Nuclear Waste," *New York Times*, 26 March 1999, 1, 17 (A); Miller, *Living in the Environment*, 12th ed., 320–357; Erikson, *A New Species*, 203–225.

86. Miller, *Living in the Environment*, 12th ed., 320–357, 368.

87. Miller, *Living in the Environment*, 12th ed., 358–394.

88. Keith Bradsher, "Fuel Economy for New Cars Is at Lowest Level Since '80." *New York Times*, 18 May 2001, 15 (A); Miller, *Living in the Environment*, 12th ed., 358–370.

89. Danny Hakim, "Tougher Rules Are Proposed for Gas Mileage," *New York Times*, 13 December 2002, 1, 6 (B); John Heilprin, "2003 Models Slip in Mileage," *Fort Wayne News-Sentinel*, 29 October 2002, 1, 4 (B).

90. Miller, *Living in the Environment*, 12th ed., 358–394, 658–686.

91. G. Tyler Miller, *Living in the Environment: Principles, Connections, and Solutions*, 9th ed. (Belmont, Calif.: Wadsworth Publishing, 1996), 350.

92. Miller, *Living in the Environment*, 12th ed., 358–394.

93. Michael Reynolds, *Earthship* (Taos, N.Mex.: Solar Survival, 1990).

94. Miller, *Living in the Environment*, 12th ed., 378, 358–394.

95. Miller, *Living in the Environment*, 12th ed., 358–394, 381.

96. Malise Simons, "Wind Turbines Are Sprouting off Europe's Shores," *New York Times*, 8 December 2002, 3 (1); Miller, *Living in the Environment*, 12th ed., 381.

97. Miller, *Living in the Environment*, 12th ed., 358–394.

5

Global Climate Change: Linking National Deliberations with International Negotiations

Contrary to modern myth, ours is a world of limits as well as opportunities. Public wisdom lies in a selective advance of opportunities without incurring the penalties of overshooting these limits. This requires a new kind of politics for which no nation can as yet claim experience.

—Lynton K. Caldwell, "International Environmental Politics: America's Response to Global Imperatives," in *Environmental Policy in the 1990s*

BACKGROUND: FOSSIL FUELS AND AIR POLLUTION

There are many serious air pollution problems associated with the use of fossil fuels. Of the six outdoor air pollutants originally regulated under the Clean Air Acts (1970, 1977, 1990) in the United States, five result from fossil fuel combustion. They include: (1) carbon monoxide, about three-fourths of which comes from the exhaust of automobiles; (2) nitrogen dioxide, which results from fossil fuels used in autos, power generation, and industry; (3) sulfur dioxide, produced largely from the burning of coal; (4) suspended particulate matter, the major portion of which comes from the combustion of coal and diesel fuels; and (5) ozone, which results from the interaction of volatile organic compounds emitted from cars and industry, and nitrogen oxides, released from the burning of fossil fuels. Except for ozone, these are all primary air pollutants that are directly discharged into the atmosphere, as a result of either human or natural activities. They also are the basis for a number of secondary air pollutants that form in the atmosphere from the chemical interaction of these and other compounds.[1]

Among the secondary air pollution problems confronting modern societies, industrial (and, later, photochemical) smog was among the first to be recognized. Industrial smog was found in cities that had cold, wet winters and relied on coal for energy production. The sulfur in the coal used in these locales combines with oxygen when combusted, producing sulfur dioxides; the sulfur dioxides then combine with suspended particulate matter to form the smog that enveloped London, Chicago, and Philadelphia in the nineteenth and early twentieth centuries and plagues many Eastern European and Asian cities today. Photochemical smog, on the other hand, is found in cities with warm, sunny climates that rely heavily on automobiles, such as Los Angeles, Denver, and Salt Lake City in the United States, and in other international urban centers, such as Sydney, Mexico City, and Buenos Aires. As gasoline in autos is combusted, nitrogen combines with oxygen to form nitrogen oxides, which later react with oxygen to produce nitrogen dioxides. In the presence of ultraviolet radiation, the nitrogen dioxides form substances such as ozone and PANS (peroxyacyl nitrates) to produce photochemical oxidants.[2]

It wasn't until the passage of the Clean Air Act of 1990 that a conscious effort was made to directly control secondary pollutants; acid rain (or acid deposition, or acid precipitation) became the first secondary air pollutant subject to regulation in the United States. There was significant debate about the cause of acid rain in the 1980s, during Ronald Reagan's presidency. Reagan and his advisors argued that more research was needed to prove that human activities were the major antecedent of acid precipitation, an argument similar to that of George W. Bush in the current debate over global warming. By the end of the 1980s, however, a strong scientific consensus had coalesced, pointing to the sulfur oxides produced from coal combustion and the nitrogen oxides produced from gasoline combustion in vehicles as the major offenders in causing acid precipitation. In the United States, sulfur oxides were (and are) still being emitted primarily by coal-burning power plants in the Midwest. The higher smokestacks mandated under the earlier Clean Air Acts meant that when the coal was combusted, the resulting sulfur dioxides were carried further up into the atmosphere, where they combined with additional oxygen to form sulfur trioxides; the sulfur trioxides then combined with water vapor to form sulfuric acid. It was this acid that entered wind currents and was deposited on northeastern lakes and forests in the United States and on southeastern sections of Canada. In Europe, it was coal burning in Eastern

European and some Western European cities that resulted in the acid precipitation over northern and Western Europe; air currents in Europe move from east to west. Acid precipitation has had devastating consequences for trees, as barks are impaired and leaves are damaged; acidified soil also leaches metals into nearby surface and underground waters. Trees weakened from acid deposition are more vulnerable to frost and disease, and the metals leached into waterways coat the lungs of aquatic species, causing their death and, eventually, lakes devoid of fish. Dying forests ("waldsterben") became synonymous with acid precipitation in Western Europe, where, for instance, one-half of the trees in the Black Forest in Germany were damaged. In the western United States, acid precipitation is linked to nitrogen dioxides from automobile emissions; these nitrogen dioxides, like sulfur dioxides, combine in the upper atmosphere with oxygen and water to produce an acid, in this case nitric acid, that is deposited east of where it is created. The Clean Air Act of 1990 provided for additional regulation of sulfur dioxides and created emissions trading policies for their reduction; such trading policies are also being considered for controlling the carbon dioxide emissions believed to be responsible for global warming.[3]

The depletion of stratospheric ozone is another secondary air pollution problem that the United States and other nations began to address in the 1980s. Research in the 1970s by U.S. chemists Sherwood Roland and Mario Molina pointed to the chlorine in human-produced compounds, especially chlorofluorocarbons (CFCs), as the chief culprit in the annual thinning of the ozone layer, particularly in the Southern Hemisphere. Chlorofluorocarbons, first manufactured in the 1930s, began to be widely used in industrialized nations after World War II as coolants in air conditioners and refrigerators, propellants in aerosol spray cans, and bubbling agents in plastic foams. These stable compounds entered into the atmosphere, where chlorine molecules began the process of thinning atmospheric ozone (O_3) by breaking it down into oxygen (O_2) and chlorine monoxide (C_{10}). Ozone depletion has been linked to increased incidence of severe sunburns, skin cancer, and cataracts, as well as the decreased productivity of forests and ocean phytoplankton. While the disappearance of the ozone layer itself is a problem, CFCs, while not a fossil fuel, are considered one of the greenhouse gases linked to global climate change. Since the attenuation of stratospheric ozone was related to the use of a discrete set of products for which substitutes were available, treaties to deal with this problem have been easier to achieve than for other global environmental problems. The most significant international agreement regarding ozone depletion was signed in Montreal in 1987; the Montreal Protocol focused on reducing CFC emissions by 35 percent between 1989 and 2000. Additional meetings in London in 1990 and Copenhagen in 1992 established funds for developing nations to also be able to deal with this concern. As a result, by 1999, the industrial production of CFCs had fallen 93 percent from the peak production of these compounds in 1989.[4]

Along with the loss of biodiversity to which it is linked, global climate change has now become one of the most critical environmental problems facing the world.[5] And the primary force behind contemporary climate change appears to be the human reliance on fossil fuels. While there are often temperature fluctuations from year to year, with a harsh winter one year followed by a milder one the next, or a torrid, dry summer followed by one that is cool and wet, global warming refers to changes in the *average* global temperature near the earth's surface. The last two decades of the twentieth century had fifteen of the warmest years on record since 1860. The warmest year on record was 1998, when the average global temperature reached 58 degrees Fahrenheit; the average global temperature from 1880 to 2001 was 56.9 degrees Fahrenheit. It is expected that with the presence of El Niño, 2003 will be as warm or warmer than 1998, another El Niño year.[6] It is true that the earth has gone through natural cycles of cooling and warming; geologists believe we are about ten thousand years into an interglacial period that will last from ten thousand to 12,500 years.[7] Yet, it is the dramatic rise in average global temperatures over so short a period of time that is causing so many scientists, political leaders, industry leaders, environmentalists, and ordinary citizens to worry. Noted biologist Edward O. Wilson observes:

> There can no longer be any reasonable doubt of global warming itself and its generally malign consequences for the environment and human economy. According to estimates based on tree rings, fossil air samples trapped in glacial ice, and other proxies, the mean surface temperatures of Earth varied by less than 2° F during most of the 10,000 years following the end of the Ice Age. Then from 1500 to 1900, it rose approximately 0.9° F, and from 1900 to the present it has increased another 0.9° F.[8]

Thus, while it took almost four hundred years for the average global temperature to rise about 1 degree, that same 1-degree change has now taken place in just the last century. Although this may not appear to be significant, scientists estimate that for each 1.8-degree-Fahrenheit change in average temperature, climate belts can shift as much as sixty to ninety miles northward.[9] In fact, two studies published in the journal *Nature* in early 2003 provide the first quantitative evidence that such shifts are already under way. A study conducted by Dr. Camille Parmesan, a biologist at the University of Texas, found that "species' ranges were tending to shift toward the poles at some four miles a decade and that spring events, like egg laying or trees' flowering, were shifting 2.3 days earlier per decade."[10]

Of course, there has been considerable debate over whether global warming is occurring and, if so, what is causing it. Nonetheless, there is a growing consensus among scientists that global warming appears to be well under way and that humans are responsible for it.[11] One study that critics of the global warming thesis have pointed to as providing evidence that such a phenomenon is not taking place was carried out by Dr. John Christy of the University of Alabama. He found that temperatures *above* the earth's surface over the last thirty years were increasing only slightly, and, in some cases, even decreasing. However, a reanalysis of the same data has found that warming does appear to be taking place in the upper atmosphere, as well as closer to the earth's surface.[12] The Intergovernmental Panel on Climate Change, created by the World Meteorological Organization and the United Nations Environment Programme in 1988, released reports in 1990, 1995, and 2001; its findings are based on the work of hundreds of experts around the world. After its second and third reports, the panel concluded that "an increasing body of observations gives a collective picture of a warming world and other changes in the climate system" and "the balance of evidence suggests a discernible human influence on climate change."[13]

There is a natural greenhouse effect that occurs when incoming solar energy is transformed by certain gases, such as carbon dioxide and water vapor, so that the waste heat that is normally reradiated back into the atmosphere is prevented from escaping. However, since the beginning of the industrial revolution, but especially since the end of World War II, there has been a dramatic increase in the presence of greenhouse gases in the earth's atmosphere. Carbon dioxide is considered to be the most significant of the greenhouse gases, accounting for about 50 to 60 percent of the current warming; scientists estimate that about three-fourths of this increased carbon dioxide comes from the consumption of fossil fuels, while the remaining 25 percent is the result of deforestation and the burning of plants and trees. The other most significant greenhouse gas is water vapor. As the atmosphere becomes warmer, more of the earth's surface water evaporates. The disruption of the hydrological cycle will have significant impacts on precipitation and the severity of storms. Global warming will also increase sea levels, as polar ice caps melt and as ocean water expands.[14] The United States' National Oceanic and Atmospheric Administration found that in the summer of 2002, more of Greenland's glacial surface had melted than in the previous twenty-four years of its monitoring.[15] A similar finding was reported about Chacaltaya Mountain in the Bolivian Andes at the end of 2002; scientists said it was likely that the glacier on top of the mountain would be gone in ten years.[16] As the earth's atmosphere becomes warmer, more heat is transferred to the polar regions. It is estimated that in the last thirty years, the average temperature at the Arctic Circle increased by 11 degrees Fahrenheit, while the Antarctic has experienced a 5-degree-Fahrenheit increase in summer temperatures and a 10-degree-Fahrenheit increase in winter temperatures since 1947.[17]

Besides carbon dioxide and water vapor, other greenhouse gases include: (1) methane, which results from the breakdown of organic matter in places such as landfills, wetlands, rice paddies, and swamps; (2) nitrous oxides, which occur from the burning of fossil fuels, the production of nylon, and the breakdown of fertilizers; and (3) chlorofluorocarbons, which are emitted from leaking air conditioners and refrigerators and the production of plastic foams. Still, the Intergovernmental Panel on Climate Change has been most concerned about the human-induced levels of carbon dioxide in the atmosphere and their role in global warming. They have predicted that if the level of carbon dioxide in the atmosphere doubles from the preindustrial level of 280 parts per million to 560 parts per million by the year 2100 (it is currently at 360 parts per million), the average global surface temperature could increase from 2.5 degrees Fahrenheit to 10.4 degrees Fahrenheit.[18] This could lead to some of the worst potential consequences of global warming, including: (1) the shift in climate belts, which could have devastating impacts on agriculture, biodiversity, and water supplies; (2) a rise in sea levels as ocean water expands, with potential calamitous consequences for the one-third of the world's population that lives along ocean coasts; (3) extreme and erratic weather patterns, including the increased intensity of hurricanes and tornadoes, increased heat waves and droughts, and increased flooding; and (4) dramatic consequences for human health, due to rising temperatures, increases in infectious diseases, disruption of food and water supplies, and elevated air and water pollution levels.[19]

NEGOTIATING LIMITS ON GREENHOUSE GASES

While some have suggested that more research needs to be done on the causes and consequences of global climate change, and others have argued in favor of doing nothing—because they believe either that global warming is not a serious threat or, if it is, that humans can learn to adapt to it—there is now a growing consensus that human beings will need to directly and actively respond to this problem.[20] This position was first cogently articulated in *Our Common Future*, the report issued by the United Nations World Commission on Environment and Development in 1987. Actually, the work of the commission, which began in 1983, can be traced back to the first United Nations Conference on the Human Environment, held in Stockholm, Sweden, in 1972. Also that year, an Environmental Action Programme was added to the Treaty of Rome, which in 1957 had created the European Economic Community—the forerunner of the present European Union. These earliest efforts to deal with the world's growing and more obvious global environmental problems culminated twenty years later in the historic second United Nations Conference on the Environment and Development, held in Rio de Janeiro, Brazil, in 1992.[21] At this conference, a United Nations Commission on Sustainable Development was proposed and the first United Nations Framework Convention on Climate Change was signed, along with several other significant initiatives.[22]

The framework was shaped by several key principles. One of these was the idea that the absence of scientific certainty about global warming should not prevent the world community from taking action to deal with it; the enormity of the consequences of not acting was too great. Furthermore, it could be argued that the movement away from fossil fuels would also be wise in any case, given their finite nature and severe pollution consequences. Another principle influencing the framework was the recognition that different countries bore different responsibilities for the current level of greenhouse gases and therefore had greater initial obligations to restrain emissions. This notion had also been articulated by the World Commission on Environment and Development. In the process of dramatically increasing their standards of living since the end of World War II, the more industrialized nations had been using the atmosphere as a "sink" for disposing of the waste products of fossil fuel combustion. By the year 2000, for instance, the United States alone was responsible for 24 percent of global carbon dioxide emissions. Moreover, these same industrialized nations had greater resources to expend on this problem. Thus, the framework called for the industrialized nations to reduce their carbon dioxide emissions to 1990 levels by the year 2000. However, objections from the George H. W. Bush administration resulted in the framework making these emission goals voluntary, and not mandatory.[23]

By 1995, the signatories to the framework had determined that these voluntary goals were ineffective; they met in Berlin (also referred to as the Conference of the Parties or COPI) to develop a new agreement, with legally binding obligations. A year later in Geneva at COPII, those nations in attendance worked on a protocol that would become the basis for the agreement signed at COPIII in Kyoto, Japan, in 1997. The Kyoto Protocol committed the industrialized nations to reducing their emissions of greenhouse gases 5.2 percent below their 1990 levels between 2008 and 2012; it committed the developing nations to more intensively monitor and develop plans for curtailing greenhouse gases. The protocol also permitted the trading of carbon dioxide emissions permits and allowed for countries to meet carbon dioxide emissions reductions by factoring in the effects of forests in removing atmospheric carbon. With pressure from environmental organizations and through the efforts of Vice President Al Gore, President Clinton signed the Kyoto Protocol. However, the Clinton administration never submitted the protocol to the Senate for ratification, fearing it would fail to receive the necessary two-thirds majority. Congressional objections to the protocol focused particularly on the differential obligations of the developed and developing nations in reducing carbon emissions.[24]

Several other Conferences of the Parties were held in the ensuing years to refine the details of the Kyoto Protocol; these included COPIV in Buenos Aires in 1998, COPV in Bonn in 1999, and COPVI at The Hague in 2000.[25] In March 2001, however, newly elected president George W. Bush announced that the United States was withdrawing from the Kyoto Protocol, citing the damage it would cause to the American economy.[26] In June 2001, a report by the National Academy of Sciences, which had been requested by the Bush administration, found that "greenhouse gases are accumulating in earth's atmosphere as a result of human activities, causing surface air temperatures and subsurface ocean temperatures to rise." The panel contained eleven prominent American atmospheric scientists, including some who had previously expressed skepticism about global warming. The report noted that "national policy decisions made now and in the longer-term future will influence the extent of any damage suffered by vulnerable human populations and ecosystems later in this century."[27] In July 2001, representatives of 178 nations, absent the United States, finalized the Kyoto Protocol in Bonn, Germany; the treaty then had to be submitted to a final ratification process. The protocol required thirty-eight industrialized nations to reduce their carbon dioxide emissions to 5.2 percent below their 1990 levels. The European Union also agreed to donate $410 million a year to developing countries to create alternative energy technologies.[28] The final details of the Kyoto Protocol were worked out in Marrakesh, Morocco, in November 2001. The treaty will not take effect, however, until it is ratified by fifty-five nations, including nations that are responsible for 55 percent of the current greenhouse emissions.[29] The Intergovernmental Panel on Climate Change estimates that even to stabilize the presence of greenhouse gases in the environment at 450 parts per million by 2100 will require a reduction of carbon dioxide emissions by 70 to 80 percent; this is a much larger reduction than will be required under the current Kyoto Protocol.[30]

In February 2002, President Bush announced his administration's strategy to deal with global warming; it focused on voluntary emissions limits encouraged by tax credits. The *New York Times* commented:

Mr. Bush's long-awaited substitute for Kyoto is a disappointment. The essence of his strategy is a concept that seems to have been minted for the occasion, called "emissions intensity," under which carbon dioxide pollution would be allowed to grow but at a slower rate than economic output. That sounds attractive, but it misses the point. The buildup of carbon dioxide in the atmosphere, already alarmingly high, is a cumulative process. Thus the name of the game is to stop adding new emissions to the vast amounts already up there, not simply to slow their growth.[31]

In June 2002, the Bush administration was required to submit a report on climate change to the United Nations; the report, prepared by the United States Environmental Protection Agency, with input from other agencies, concluded that the global climate was undergoing serious changes as the result of human-produced pollution.[32] However, several days after the report was issued, President Bush said, "I read the report put out by the bureaucracy." He noted again his opposition to the Kyoto Protocol and argued that voluntary efforts were the best approach to curb greenhouse emissions.[33] When the Bush administration issued its annual federal report on air pollution in September 2002, global warming was not mentioned, the first time that the report had not addressed that issue since 1996.[34] Toward the end of 2002, the Bush administration reversed long-term policy commitments in two areas that also had significant implications for global warming: clean air regulations and national forest rules.

The Bush administration decided not to require industry, power plants, and utilities to meet current clean air requirements when they underwent repairs or expansion; the "new source review program" had been developed over ten years as part of the Clean Air Act. It mandated that aging facilities, many of which had been exempt from the Clean Air Act since 1977, had to meet the newest clean air requirements once the facilities were updated. Several plants already were being sued by the United States Environmental Protection Agency (suits begun under the Clinton administration) for failure to meet the newest standards. At the end of November 2002, the Bush administration announced that it would issue new regulations that would end new source review, thus allowing these older plants to continue to emit high levels of sulfur oxides, nitrogen oxides, and carbon dioxide. The rationale offered by the Bush administration was that the new source review program discouraged industries from updating their equipment, and this alternative approach would allow industry to voluntarily comply with higher standards. Several governors and attorney generals from northeastern states said they would sue the EPA over its abandonment of the new source review program.[35]

The second set of policy changes the Bush administration undertook at the end of 2002 (some analysts noted these changes followed the 2002 elections, when the Republicans regained control of the Senate and maintained their control of the House) focused on three issues related to the National Forests. The first, more an act of omission than commission, involved the Bush administration's failure to defend a court challenge to the "roadless rules." These rules had been developed under the Clinton administration and involved sixty million acres in the National Forests that would be protected from logging, mining, and oil drilling. The second initiative involved the speeding up of environmental reviews in the National Forests to allow for forest thinning to prevent wildfires. Critics of this policy worried that this change would further shift National Forest Service policy away from concern with environmental values, as would a third initiative that would allow forest managers in the National Forests much greater discretion to allow logging and other commercial activities without doing the environmental impact studies that had previously been required.[36] Thus, the Bush administration was not only abandoning what some considered a rather limited, and not at all radical, approach to global warming with its withdrawal from the Kyoto Protocol, but it was also administratively implementing changes to rules about air pollution and forest protection that would likely increase America's contributions to the global warming problem.

CREATING OPPORTUNITIES TO DISCUSS, PARTICIPATE IN, AND DELIBERATE NATIONAL ENERGY AND GLOBAL CLIMATE CHANGE POLICIES

Changes, perhaps fundamental ones, may be needed in political, social, and economic institutions, as well as in how we reason together about ethical commitments, in order to create the conditions for adequately comprehending, discussing, participating in, and deliberating over our responsibilities in the global environmental community. In terms of the nation's traditional political institutions, there is a clear role for both political parties and interest groups in redirecting the nation's policies toward those that are more eco-centric and globally focused. It was in fact interest groups devoted to environmental and social justice issues in the late 1960s, and the eventual response of the nation's political parties, Congress, presidents, and executive agencies, that helped to usher in the "environmental decade" of the 1970s. Analysts such as Allan Schnaiberg and Kenneth Alan Gould[37] argue that the environmental movement of the 1960s was at its core a social movement based in the middle class; it was the strong presence and intense concern of this segment of the American population that provoked such a sweeping response. Of course, American citizens, even the majority who express anxieties about our environmental future, hold differing views about what exactly we should be doing as a nation to more effectively secure it.[38] These orientations range from those who argue for a radical restructuring of our economic and social institutions, to those who see the need for incremental reforms that could be accomplished through existing mechanisms, to those who think an awakened consumer consciousness and environmental education are the key. And of course, there are those Americans for whom environmental problems are negligible or nonexistent, and who see no reason to change any of our current practices. Clearly, however, there is a relationship between citizens becoming more concerned about these environmental problems and the election of leaders who are motivated to move the country in new directions. At the same time, and as has happened throughout our history, a bold and courageous leader can also take the country in directions it seemed reluctant to go without such guidance. Abraham Lincoln and Franklin Delano Roosevelt steered the country in uncharted and historically significant directions; they are ranked consistently by presidential scholars as among the greatest presidents. In Arthur Schlesinger Jr.'s last poll, in 1996, only three presidents were rated as great by American historians: George Washington, Abraham Lincoln, and Franklin Delano Roosevelt.[39]

Yet, at a more fundamental level, the argument can be made that we as a nation are in danger of losing our way; that citizens are not deeply engaged in choosing the future directions of our society and that those directions are not being informed by a reasonable set of ethical commitments.[40] For the emergence of what I am calling the "democratically derived realm of civil ethics," the actual involvement of the American populace in discussions, in actions, and in deliberations about our environmental future may be necessary. In his book *Strong Democracy*,[41] Benjamin Barber proposes a three-tiered schema for characterizing democracies according to how their citizens participate in policy decisions. He begins with direct democracy, the oldest model of self-rule, which characterized the Greek city-states, in which *all* citizens (of course, a rather limited constituency at the time) participated in *all* decisions *all* of the time. This model was largely superseded in the eighteenth century by representative democracies, in which *all* citizens (at this nation's beginning, also a limited group) elect *some* people (our representatives) who then make *all* of the key political decisions. There are many reasons that the founders developed a representative, rather than a direct, form of democracy in America. These include not only the impracticality of direct participation in a nation with a geographically dispersed citizenry, but also the founders' fear of a mass electorate, whose desires, conflicts, and interests, they believed, needed to be mediated by fragmenting governing institutions; power was divided between the national government and the states, and a division of powers was also created at the national level between a two-house legislature and the executive and judicial branches. This model could temper passions and ensure that changes would be incremental. And while this has provided the nation with political stability, it has also created the conditions under which the electorate is increasingly distant from the decisions being made in its name.[42] Add to this the decisive turn to liberal proceduralism in the late 1930s,[43] whereby, in order to incorporate a growing and diverse electorate, governmental policies became increasingly focused on providing fair procedures, equal protection of rights, and a neutral stance toward value orientations. Barber calls the resulting contemporary democratic institutions "thin," and proposes a third model, which he calls "strong democracy"; it is predicated on the notion that a reinvigorated democracy will require the increased involvement of citizens.

Barber's strong democracy is premised on a system in which *all* of the citizens become involved in *some* of the decisions *some* of the time. While direct democracy is impractical under modern conditions, and representative democracy appears to be inadequate, a strong democracy would engage citizens in a variety of opportunities to talk, participate in, and make decisions about the country's future; policy directions would be informed by their input. Citizens would choose the realm in which or the level at which they wished to be involved. This model obviously depends on a citizenry that wants to participate. Juliet B. Schor[44] and others argue that a society that engaged our civic energies, valued participation, consciously decided to set limits on working hours, de-emphasized the value of ever-expanding production and consumption activities—and instead reached a "steady-state,"[45] such that wealth and population were maintained at sustainable levels through the efficient use of matter and energy—would provide its citizens with the time and the desire to toil in the vineyards of the common good. Americans, despite contemporary concerns about the decline in civic participation,[46] still volunteer their time and talents in very extensive and generous ways that are characteristic of a vibrant civil society.[47] Increased opportunities for direct participation in defining the nation's future could replace the passive and ersatz culture that threatens to alienate us from each other, our communities, our nation, and the world.

This presents us with the challenge then of reengaging citizens in defining the direction of the nation and deliberating about the ethical values that will guide it. Such involvement could be realized in three different loci. The first could include more opportunities for face-to-face discussions among citizens in order to learn about and to form policy preferences about a variety of environmental issues. These discussions could take place in settings such as neighborhood assemblies, as Barber[48] suggests. And while these forums may naturally begin with a focus on local concerns, they most probably will lead to discussions of their regional, national, and even international implications. Such assemblies could represent the best of neighbors meeting, talking to each other, hearing from a variety of experts and interest groups, and developing the beginnings of policy options. These policy options may or may not be linked to local governing institutions. In addition to talking, Barber and others[49] discuss the need to have citizens actually participate in activities in which they learn about common interests by working alongside others. For environmental issues, something along the lines of the Civilian Conservation Corps might provide a model. From the young, who might be given credits toward college tuition, to retired citizens, whose involvement would provide physical and emotional benefits, a variety of environmental rehabilitation, education, and demonstration projects could be undertaken. Participation may also mean involvement in organizations and agencies that have environmental missions. This participation obviously could take place at the local, state, regional, national, or international level.

Finally, we need to provide opportunities for citizens to actively be engaged in decision making about the environment. Here Barber suggests mechanisms such as referendums and even electronic balloting. Both are examples of direct participation, but they represent an adversarial form of democracy in which citizens' interests are assumed to be in conflict.[50] Another alternative is to have citizens formally deliberate with each other on environmental policy options, in order to uncover potential common interests. Participants on these bodies could be chosen at random, along the lines of the minipopulus suggested by Dahl,[51] or they could be selected to represent specific interests, including geographic regions, occupational categories, or environmental orientations. These deliberations could take place on the local, state, regional, or national level. They would involve uncovering value commitments and understanding how policies lead to or away from them. Herschel Elliott and Richard Lamm suggest the importance of this type of deliberation, after raising questions about whether the type of unlimited growth that undergirds the American economy is sustainable. They ask:

> What if such a scenario is unsustainable? What if we need an ethics for a finite world, an ethics of the commons? It is not important that you agree with the premise. What is important is that you help debate the alternatives. An ethics of the commons would require a change in the criteria by which moral claims are justified.[52]

These deliberations would take place in the public sphere, where individuals would have to justify their reasons to each other. They may lead to an understanding of limits and responsibilities that may be said to constitute the realm of civil ethics. Again Elliott and Lamm:

> You may believe that current rates of population growth and economic expansion can go on forever—but debate with us what alternative ethical theories would arise if they cannot. Our thesis is that any ethical system is mistaken and immoral if its practice would cause an environmental collapse.[53]

The deliberations could be linked directly to the formal institutions of governance, which have the power to ultimately make decisions on these subjects. For instance, in the case of our energy future or global warming policies, citizen representatives could deliberate over an extended period of time in order to develop policy preferences that could be brought either to state legislatures or the Congress, or to state governors or the president. The beginning of discussion, participation, and deliberation on these issues would provide the groundwork, hopefully, for our international involvement in these issues, as well. The United States, which in the 1970s was seen as leader on global environmental issues, had its secretary of state, Colin Powell, booed at the World Summit on Sustainable Development, held in Johannesburg, South Africa, from August 26 to September 4, 2002.[54] We seem to have forfeited the goodwill with which the world regarded the United States, especially after World War II, and now appear unwilling to cooperatively work with other nations, except on our own terms and only when it benefits us.[55] In fact, Michael Ignatieff notes that the face of the American to people around the world is now a soldier, as our share of humanitarian and social assistance to other nations has declined, while our military investments and commitments have risen. The United States contributed 0.2 percent of its gross national product (GNP) to other nations for assistance in 1992, which dropped to 0.1 percent in 2002. In comparison, Denmark contributed 1.02 percent of its GNP toward assistance to developing countries in 1992, which increased to 1.06 percent in 2000. In 2000, the United States was behind fourteen other industrialized nations in the percentage of our GNP we devoted to assistance, including Denmark, the Netherlands, Sweden, Norway, Belgium, Switzerland, France, the United Kingdom, Japan, Germany, Australia, Canada, Spain, and Italy.[56] Part of what we may need to recover then, in the United States, is an understanding of our ethical commitments and responsibilities to one another, to the other humans with whom we currently share the planet, to future generations who will occupy the planet, and to other species, present and future, which are vital parts of the biosphere. We need to discuss, participate in, and deliberate with each other over environmental policy directions and goals; those undertakings may then help us to uncover and begin to more seriously evaluate our common ethical biospheric commitments. These commitments may then provide linkages to the policies, actions, and goals that we want to implement with other nations. The reasons we might want to foster opportunities for citizens to discuss, participate in, and deliberate about policy issues and to become more fully engaged in the ethical directions of the nation are the subject of the last chapter.

NOTES

1. G. Tyler Miller Jr., *Living in the Environment: Principles, Connections, and Solutions*, 12th ed. (Belmont, Calif.: Wadsworth/Thomson Learning, 2002), 417–445.

2. Miller, *Living in the Environment*, 417–445.

3. Sandra Postel, "Air Pollution, Acid Rain, and Forests," *State of the World 1985* (New York: Norton, 1985), 123–140; Miller, *Living in the Environment*, 417–445.

4. Miller, *Living in the Environment*, 446–475.

5. Edward O. Wilson, *The Future of Life* (New York: Knopf, 2002); Andrew C. Revkin, "Warming Is Found to Disrupt Species," *New York Times*, 2 January 2003, 15 (A).

6. Miller, *Living in the Environment*, 446–475; Andrew C. Revkin, "Temperatures Are Likely to Go from Warm to Warmer," *New York Times*, 31 December 2002, 3 (D).

7. Miller, *Living in the Environment*, 446–475.

8. Wilson, *The Future of Life*, 67.

9. Miller, *Living in the Environment*, 446–475.

10. Revkin, "Warming Is Found," 15 (A).

11. Miller, *Living in the Environment*, 446–475; Wilson, *The Future of Life*; Seth Dunn and Christopher Flavin, "Moving the Climate Change Agenda Forward," in *State of the World 2002*, ed. Linda Starke (New York: Norton, 2002), 24–50; Revkin, "Temperatures"; Gary C. Bryner, *Gaia's Wager: Environmental Movements and the Challenge of Sustainability* (Lanham, Md.: Rowman & Littlefield, 2001); Peter Wenz, "Justice, Democracy, and Global Warming," in *Democracy and the Claims of Nature: Critical Perspectives for a New Century*, ed. Ben A. Minteer and Bob Pepperman Taylor (Lanham, Md.: Rowman & Littlefield, 2002), 191–214.

12. Revkin, "Temperatures."

13. Dunn and Flavin, "Moving the Climate Change Agenda Forward."

14. Miller, *Living in the Environment*, 446–475; Dunn and Flavin, "Moving the Climate Change Agenda Forward."

15. Revkin, "Temperatures."

16. "Shrinking Glaciers," editorial, *New York Times*, 1 December 2002, 8 (4).

17. Miller, *Living in the Environment*, 446–475.

18. Miller, *Living in the Environment*, 446–475; Dunn and Flavin, "Moving the Climate Change Agenda Forward."

19. Miller, *Living in the Environment*, 446–475; Dunn and Flavin, "Moving the Climate Change Agenda Forward"; Gary Gardner, "The Challenge for Johannesburg: Creating a More Secure World," in *State of the World 2002*, ed. Linda Starke, 3–23.

20. Miller, *Living in the Environment*, 446–475; Dunn and Flavin, "Moving the Climate Change Agenda Forward"; Hilary French, "Reshaping Global Governance," in *State of the World 2002*, ed. Linda Starke, 174–198; Janet Sawin, "Charting a New Energy Future," in *State of the World 2003*, ed. Linda Starke (New York: Norton, 2003), 85–109; Wilson, *The Future of Life*; Katherine Q. Seelye and Andrew C. Revkin, "Panel Tells Bush Global Warming Is Getting Worse," *New York Times*, 7 June 2001, 1, 25 (A).

21. Regina S. Axelrod, "Environmental Policy and Management in the European Union," in *Environmental Policy in the 1990s*, 3rd ed., ed. Norman J. Vig and Michael E. Kraft (Washington, D.C.: Congressional Quarterly, 1997), 299–320; Marvin S. Soroos, "From Stockholm to Rio and Beyond: The Evolution of Global Environmental Governance," in *Environmental Policy in the 1990s*, 3rd ed., 278–298.

22. Miller, *Living in the Environment*, 732–737; Dunn and Flavin, "Moving the Climate Change Agenda Forward"; French, "Reshaping Global Governance." A draft of the Framework Convention on Climate Change was drawn up in 1991 by an International Negotiating Committee under the auspices of the United Nations; see Marvin S. Soroos, "Negotiating Our Climate," in *Global Climate Change*, ed. Sharon L. Spray and Karen L. McGlothlin (Lanham, Md.: Rowman & Littlefield, 2002), 121–144.

23. Dunn and Flavin, "Moving the Climate Change Agenda Forward."

24. Dunn and Flavin, "Moving the Climate Change Agenda Forward"; Bryner, *Gaia's Wager*; Soroos, "Negotiating Our Climate."

25. Soroos, "Negotiating Our Climate."

26. Douglas Jehl, "U.S. Going Empty-Handed to Meeting on Global Warming," *New York Times*, 29 March 2001, 19 (A).

27. Seelye and Revkin, "Panel Tells Bush."

28. Andrew C. Revkin, "Global Warming Impasse Is Broken." *New York Times*, 11 November 2001, 8 (A).

29. Revkin, "Global Warming Impasse Is Broken."

30. Dunn and Flavin, "Moving the Climate Change Agenda Forward."

31. "Backward on Global Warming," editorial, *New York Times*, 16 February 2002, 18 (A).

32. Andrew C. Revkin, "U.S. Pollution Report Omits Section on Global Warming," *New York Times*, 15 September 2002, 16 (A).

33. Katherine Q. Seelye, "President Distances Himself from Global Warming Report," *New York Times*, 5 June 2002, at wysiyg://34/http://www.nytimes.com.

34. Revkin, "U.S. Pollution Report." As this book is being completed, a front-page article in the 19 June 2003 *New York Times* reported that a "comprehensive review" to be issued by the Environmental Protection Agency in late June 2003,

which examines the state of knowledge on a variety of environmental issues, deleted "a long section describing risks from rising global temperatures" after it was edited by "the White House." Furthermore, "an April 29 memorandum circulated among [EPA] staff members said that after the changes by White House officials, the section on climate change 'no longer accurately represents scientific consensus on climate change.'" See Andrew C. Revkin and Katherine Q. Seelye, "White House Cuts Data on Warming in an E.P.A. Report," *New York Times*, 19 June 2003, 1, 21 (A).

35. Christopher Marquis, "Bush Energy Proposal Seeks to 'Clear Skies,'" *New York Times*, 30 July 2002, 10 (A); Matthew Wald, "EPA Says It Will Change Rules Governing Industrial Pollution," *New York Times*, 23 November 2002, 1, 16 (A).

36. Robert Pear, "Bush Plan Gives More Discretion to Forest Managers on Logging," *New York Times*, 28 November 2002, 1, 27 (A); Katherine Q. Seelye, "Bush Proposes Changes to Allow More Thinning of Forests," *New York Times*, 12 December 2002, 32 (A); Douglas Jehl, "Court Reinstates Ban on Building Forest Roads," *New York Times*, 13 December 2002, 21 (A).

37. Allan Schnaiberg, *The Environment: From Surplus to Scarcity* (New York: Oxford University Press, 1980); Allan Schnaiberg and Kenneth Alan Gould, *Environment and Society: The Enduring Conflict* (New York: St. Martin's, 1994).

38. Schnaiberg, *The Environment*; Schnaiberg and Gould, *Environment and Society*; John Dryzek, *The Politics of the Earth: Environmental Discourses* (New York: Oxford University Press, 1997); Christopher J. Bosso, "Environmental Groups and the New Political Landscape," in *Environmental Policy*, 4th ed., ed. Norman J. Vig and Michael E. Kraft (Washington, D.C.: Congressional Quarterly, 2000), 55–76; Robert C. Paehlke, "Environmental Values and Public Policy," in *Environmental Policy*, 4th ed., 77–97.

39. James Lindgren, "Rating the Presidents of the United States, 1789–2000: A Survey of Scholars in History, Political Science, and Law," *Federalist Society and Wall Street Journal*, 16 November 2000.

40. Michael Sandel, *Democracy's Discontent: America in Search of a Public Philosophy* (Cambridge, Mass.: Belknap Press of Harvard University, 1996); Robert Dahl, *Controlling Nuclear Weapons: Democracy versus Guardianship* (New York: Syracuse University Press, 1985); Herschel Elliott and Richard Lamm, "A Moral Code for a Finite World," *The Chronicle Review*, 15 November 2002, 7–9 (B).

41. Benjamin Barber, *Strong Democracy: Participatory Politics for a New Age* (Berkeley: University of California Press, 1984).

42. Dahl, *Controlling Nuclear Weapons*.

43. Sandel, *Democracy's Discontent*, 3–24, 250–274.

44. Juliet B. Schor, *The Overworked American: The Unexpected Decline of Leisure* (New York: Basic, 1991); Robert D. Putnam, *Bowling Alone: The Collapse and Revival of American Community* (New York: Simon & Schuster, 2000); Todd Rakoff, *A Time for Every Purpose: Law and the Balance of Life* (Cambridge, Mass.: Harvard University Press, 2002); Paul L. Wachtel, *The Poverty of Affluence: A Psychological Portrait of the American Way of Life* (Philadelphia, Pa.: New Society, 1989).

45. Herman E. Daly, *Beyond Growth* (Boston: Beacon, 1996); Elliott and Lamm, "Moral Code."

46. Putnam, *Bowling Alone*.

47. Everett Carll Ladd, *The Ladd Report* (New York: Free Press, 1999).

48. Barber, *Strong Democracy*.

49. Sandel, *Democracy's Discontent*; Ted Bernard and Jora Young, *The Ecology of Hope: Communities Collaborate for Sustainability* (Gabriola Island, British Columbia: New Society, 1997); Craig A. Rimmerman, *The New Citizenship: Unconventional Politics, Activism, and Service* (Boulder, Colo.: Westview, 1997); Richard C. Box, *Citizen Governance: Leading American Communities into the 21st Century* (Thousand Oaks, Calif.: Sage, 1998).

50. Jane Mansbridge, *Beyond Adversary Democracy* (Chicago: University of Chicago Press, 1983).

51. Dahl, *Controlling Nuclear Weapons*.

52. Elliott and Lamm, "Moral Code," 8 (B).

53. Elliott and Lamm, "Moral Code," 8 (B).

54. James Dao, "Protesters Interrupt Powell Speech as U.N. Talks End," *New York Times*, 5 September 2002, 8 (A).

55. Michael Ignatieff, "The Burden," *New York Times Magazine*, 5 January 2003, 22; Joseph S. Nye Jr., *The Paradox of American Power: Why the World's Only Superpower Can't Go It Alone* (New York: Oxford University Press, 2002).

56. French, "Reshaping Global Governance."

6

Conclusion: Learning to Share the Future

The Earth is one but the world is not.

—The World Commission on Environment and Development,
Our Common Future

One of the central concerns of this book has been to understand how complex, industrialized societies, such as the United States, can foster values and develop institutions that promote democratic discussion about, participation in, and deliberation over our environmental future, as well as forge a civil ethos capable of guiding behavior, goals, and policies about the biosphere. As the nature of modern communities has changed and relationships within the modern polity have languished, opportunities for face-to-face conversations over key issues, participation in related activities and programs, and deliberation over public plans and ideals have diminished. Such endeavors, if supported, could inform our legislation and principles and affect our willingness to work with other nations on these issues. Proposals for linking citizens in communities and throughout the polity to the public sphere(s), governmental sector(s), and a realm of civil ethics raise fundamental issues about their desirability and viability, however. Given that Americans have greatly benefited from the freedom to pursue their own notions of the good in the private sphere, especially during the last half of the twentieth century, should we even be concerned about the possible attenuation of shared public commitments at this point in our history?[1] And, even if a case could be made that it would be beneficial to enhance our understanding of the commonweal and translate this into statutes and precepts, is it even possible in twenty-first-century America to create opportunities and institutions to accomplish this?

Let us first consider why developing a more robust and politically relevant public sphere and governmental sector, supported by a democratically derived realm of civil ethics, might be desirable. Americans have garnered real advantages from the increased opportunities to construct their own paths to the good life. This is the triumph of classic liberalism in the United States and the consecration of the procedural republican ideal.[2] More than perhaps at any other point in our history, the focus on the satisfaction of individual interests (over the fulfillment of communal goals), and the increased capacity of at least some portion of the American populace to purchase the accoutrements of uniquely constructed lifestyles, have propelled the American dream.[3] By abandoning efforts to involve the citizenry in publicly deliberating over policy directions or in developing or being governed by a shared civil ethos, at least some of the attendant problems of a diverse polity have been addressed. Especially as the nation became more cognizant of its increased heterogeneity in the period following World War II, and finally open to the need to expand the polity to include previously marginalized individuals and groups, it depended on procedural liberalism[4] to help dissipate conflict and promote tolerance. This approach lessened tensions by focusing on the fulfillment of individual interests (with continued dissension, however, over whether opportunities to pursue interests were in fact equal), while pushing the discussion of common concerns and shared values outside the public sphere.[5] More than in previous eras, engaged participation and moral discourse were relegated to the organizations and institutions of the private sphere. The contemporary search for meaning and attachment now winds through the realms of family, an array of community, religious, and voluntary associations, and into the world of work;[6] at the same time, these institutions have themselves been undergoing profound changes that, depending on one's perspective, have helped to liberate or weaken them. Their formative role in the development of what an earlier age saw as the shaping of character and the embrace of civic obligations has declined.[7] The burden (or opportunity) is now placed on individuals themselves to navigate these arenas in order to construct a coherent and meaningful universe.[8] While work has become an important locus for some in the search for identity and community,[9] the increasingly unequal distribution of wealth and life opportunities in the United States, and the experiences of many in the last two decades with corporations that seem to have little commitment to them or surrounding communities, make work as a site of significant integrative experiences quite problematic.[10]

More direct participation in policy and more formalized deliberation over civil ethics are now inhibited through our nation's reliance on an adversarial form of democracy and a value-neutral orientation in governmental institutions and constitutional practice.[11] Let us first consider some of the consequences of limiting direct citizen involvement in policy making in the public sphere and governmental sector, before turning to issues that arise from the failure to address underlying values and correlative ethics in public discourse and planning. Mansbridge argues that the core assumptions of adversary democracies, which emerged along with nation-states and laissez-faire economies in the seventeenth and eighteenth centuries, accord well with the basic tenets of classical liberal philosophy. Particularly as nations such as the United States became larger and more complex, an approach to political decision making that assumed that individuals' interests were likely to be in conflict, and that competition in the political marketplace would allow citizens to choose who could best represent them in formal decision making, had great appeal. Representatives, after debate from contending positions, could then fashion decisions through majority rule. While representatives and citizens agree to disagree, in both the polity and the society, moral weight is lent to choices when at least 50 percent of the participants support them. Mansbridge believes that adversary democracy is likely to remain the dominant form of decision making in the United States, precisely because our society is so large and diverse; nonetheless, she notes that the singular reliance on this approach limits the nation's opportunities to explore policy options based on common interests, particularly for subjects that might concern responsibility for others or dedication to underlying principles. It is largely in the private sphere, in the institutions of the family and civil society, that unitary democracy—based on the assumption of common interests, face-to-face decision making, and consensus—is more likely to be found. Mansbridge argues that there could be many more opportunities to hone our unitary skills and discover our shared concerns in neighborhood organizations, workplace settings, and voluntary associations than there are currently.[12]

By failing to even attempt to explore common interests in some crucial areas of policy making, we may not be pursuing the best course for our nation, particularly if we are at all concerned about the longer-term and ethical implications of our actions. Instead, we tend to debate from fixed positions, generally preferring short-term goals and economic efficiency. When we don't consider the broadest range of options in policy discussions, we may not be making the best decisions. The more information brought to consultations and the more seriously the implications are evaluated from a variety of perspectives, the more efficacious decisions are likely to be.[13] Moreover, when the diversity of participants and viewpoints is accorded a place in decision making, the outcomes of those deliberations are more likely to be seen as legitimate, even among those whose preferences have not prevailed.[14] Finally, as Dahl notes, our tendency to delegate more and more crucial decisions to experts, governmental agencies, organized interests, and, ultimately, our elected representatives means that citizens are participating less and less in the central decisions facing our nation and the world. This transfer of authority has occurred for a number of reasons, including the growing technical complexity of the subjects, the time commitment serious participation would require, and the vast array of distractions that our material culture provides. The result is a democracy that is increasingly fragile, hollow, and seeming to move away from the citizenry's control.[15]

At the same time, the focus on value neutrality in the public sphere, governmental sector, and constitutional discourse prevents the emergence of shared ethics that might guide our policies. While this approach lessens conflicts in our society and promotes a certain level of tolerance, an attainment that should not be minimized, it also has serious drawbacks. The things that we hold most dear are not central to our experiences in the public realm. We mask our most deeply held beliefs and relegate one another to the status of "rights-bearing" individuals, not full human beings worthy of respect.[16] We are unable to plan our futures together with any sense of responsibility for our fellow Americans or for the others with whom we share the planet. Instead, the good is whatever emerges from the rancor of a particular policy debate, later to be upended by another resolution arising from a new coalition of interests that manages to hold sway. At its best this liberal pluralist approach is dependent on an even playing field; the power of ideas to win converts, and not the influence of money to convert allies, is supposed to be central. Those conditions are increasingly problematic to ensure in the funds-driven political culture of late-twentieth- and early-twenty-first-century America.[17] Yet even beyond that huge impediment to genuine deliberation based on reasoning in the public sphere, an emphasis on value neutrality doesn't necessarily produce value-neutral policies. It only eliminates the need to explicitly acknowledge the values that undergird our positions and the ethical implications of the approaches we take. It often leaves participants angry because their real concerns are not addressed during discussions; it also leaves them distrustful of a process in which parties appear to be acting in bad faith or dishonest about their intentions. This makes it difficult to establish a shared framework within which to judge the ethical implications of our actions, prevents us from adopting longer-term planning outlooks, and inhibits us from asking too much of our citizens, communities, or nation.[18] The kinds of issues that may be most important for our future may require something of us; they may necessitate limits on our behavior and restraints on our actions. If we are to embark on such undertakings, there will need to be some level of consensus about the desirability of the goals we want to achieve.

This may require a new type of social contract, one that deals not only with the processes by which we arrive at important decisions, but with the values that guide our plans. Both means and ends may have to be governed by what Eastern philosophers have called the "middle way" and Western philosophers the "golden mean."[19] We must find the grounds from which we can evaluate options between the endpoints of divergent positions, while at the same time developing ethical criteria located between rigidly held beliefs and no beliefs at all. Let us first consider what might constitute the middle way in terms of deliberations in the public sphere and governmental sector. Fisher and Ury point out that policy debates often are not about what they appear to be; participants may become adversarial as a result of perceived threats to their basic interests rather than substantive differences. Apprehensions may arise over issues of security, economic well-being, belonging, recognition, and control over one's life.[20] However, when we begin to move away from adamantly adhered-to positions, and instead think about the longer-term interests that may motivate individuals or groups, new solutions may emerge. For example, if we conducted an honest deliberation about the Arctic National Wildlife Refuge in Alaska and whether drilling for oil should be permitted there, the concerns of contending sides might become more clear. Proponents of drilling might be most worried about continued dependence on foreign nations for oil, or may be troubled about the economic impacts on local and state constituencies if drilling is prohibited. Opponents of the drilling may be disquieted about the disruption of critical habitats that such drilling might cause, and may have intense anxieties about what continued reliance on fossil fuels might mean for the stability of the world's climate and the integrity of the earth's ecosystems. It is at least conceivable in this case that if the parties to the discussion moved away from positions, and instead looked at their fears, hopes, and perhaps common interests in the subject, some new options might emerge. For instance, a discussion about the need for the nation to seriously invest in energy efficiency and alternative forms of renewable energy might provide a common ground on which to create new employment and future job security for local and state populations, while protecting fragile habitats and moving away from the energy sources at the heart of global warming. Arriving at such a perspective, however, would depend on having adequate time to study the matter; experts present who could shed light on the economic, social, political, and ecological impacts of various policy initiatives, both in the near and far term; and representatives of key constituencies who could provide additional insights on the subject. In order for it to succeed, those involved in the deliberation would have to genuinely be acting in good faith and honestly searching for the best answer to the policy questions before them.

Is there a point beyond which consensus should not be sought? In this regard, Amy Gutmann and Dennis Thompson[21] make the crucial distinction between deliberative and nondeliberative disagreements in political and policy conflicts. Deliberative disagreements, such as the one suggested above, involve individuals who may differ on policy options, but who can respect and understand how others might arrive at a different position. Deliberative disagreements can, if handled well, allow the parties to the dispute to investigate a larger range of alternatives than might have otherwise been the case. Nondeliberative disagreements arise, however, when the policy stance of one's opponents is so anathema to one's ethics or morals that no policy compromise is acceptable. This might include, in general policy discussions, any approach that would condone discrimination or hatred based on race, religion, nationality, disability status, or sexual orientation. In environmental policy disputes, nondeliberative disagreements could arise, for example, if a policy advocated willfully imposing torture on an animal species or unnecessary suffering on humans in order to achieve its objectives. Each individual in the debate would have to decide for him- or herself whether, under such circumstances, deliberations could proceed. If there were no basis for continued discussions, then the parties would have to leave behind the effort to try to fashion a consensus and move instead to the methods that characterize adversary decision making, including majority rule and secret ballots.[22]

This brings us to what the middle way might look like in the realm of civil ethics. Here again, a distinction would have to be made between deliberative disagreements and nondeliberative disagreements. In ethical issues related to environmental policy, deliberative disagreements could emerge over how different religious or philosophical traditions regard the diversity of life on the planet. In some religious or philosophical systems, humans receive the highest acclaim, while others honor all species. There may be nothing in the different orientations, however, that prevents discussions from exploring the ethics of respect for humans in all their known variety and species in all their known diversity. This may be distinguished from traditions that accord moral worth only to humans, and even more exclusively, only to those who adhere to a certain set of beliefs. Such exclusionary precepts could prevent deliberation from proceeding on a shared ethics for the future. However, if enough philosophical and religious canons were represented in such discussions, and if the participants could at least respect how others arrived at their beliefs, shared ethics might be uncovered that are capable of providing some guidance for the United States as it enters the twenty-first century. This may take some time to develop for these discussions, debates, and deliberations to proceed through the discursive and reflexive channels of the family, community, the economy, civil society, the public sphere, the governmental sector, and the constitutional realm. It may take time for there to be a willingness to think about these issues and to move toward some understanding of their importance in shaping our actions, limiting our behavior, and informing our public goals. We will need fuller discussion, participation, and deliberation so that what emerges out of all this activity is a conception that such an ethics may be crucial for our survival on this planet. The Dalai Lama observes:

> Fortunately, more and more people recognize the importance of ethical discipline as a means of ensuring a healthy place to live. For this reason I am optimistic that disaster can be averted. Until comparatively recently, few people gave much thought to the effects of human activity on our planet. Yet today there are even political parties whose main concern it is. Moreover, the fact that the air we breathe, the water we drink, the forests and oceans which sustain millions of different life forms, and the climatic patterns which govern our weather systems all transcend national boundaries is a source of hope. It means that no country, no matter how rich and powerful or how poor and weak it may be, can afford not to take action in respect to this issue.[23]

At least four areas of concern seem worth our deliberative time. They are the responsibilities humans have for: (1) others with whom we presently share the planet, (2) future generations, (3) other species, and (4) developing cooperative relationships with other nations to address these issues.[24] The emergence of a civil ethics would represent the triumph of the middle way in that we would be developing guideposts in the relationship of humans to the biosphere between deeply held private beliefs and no articulated set of public beliefs. These principles may help in deciding which policy questions to address, the range of options we might want to consider, and the values that should accompany us along the way. Besides the environment, there may be a number of areas that could benefit from such deliberative practices in the public sphere, the governmental sector, and the realm of civil ethics, including planning for a global and sustainable economy and issues of human rights, health care, and international governance.

Even if one accepted the argument that these proposals might prove beneficial for the tenor of community and the polity in contemporary America, they may still seem wildly impractical. At least four issues would have to be addressed before such proposals could even begin to be realized. First, there is the willingness of Americans to engage in discussions, activities, and deliberations about environmental policies and biospheric ethics. Although Americans still participate in civil society to a significant degree,[25] how could or why would citizens now take the time to engage in additional efforts focused on environmental concerns in the public sphere, governmental sector, and realm of civil ethics? Yet as the case of the Adams Center Landfill (chapter 3) illustrates, and the cases of other communities facing serious environmental problems suggest,[26] citizens are often willing to expend enormous amounts of time and effort when they understand the impacts that such issues will have on their lives. This signifies that at least one of the barriers to engaging citizens in environmental deliberations may be their lack of awareness about the relevance of these issues for their lives, their children, their communities, their states, and the nation. Particularly concerning subjects whose consequences are likely to be longer-term, such as energy policy and global climate change strategies, this becomes an important issue. In addition to a lack of consciousness about these issues, there are structural impediments to more fully engaging citizens in policy deliberations and ethical exchanges. Americans' lives are now tightly organized around routines of work and consumption.[27] The dilemma here of course is that, until Americans consciously address the lack of balance in their lives between work and all other commitments, and willfully move toward a more steady-state, sustainable economy, they are unlikely to have the time or sense of civic obligation needed to devote to such endeavors.[28] This is clearly a pivotal issue that will itself perhaps need to be the subject of face-to-face discussions, program engagements, and policy and ethical deliberations.

There is secondly the issue of information. In all of the activities suggested herein, citizens can participate meaningfully only to the extent that they have sufficient information, from a variety of perspectives, provided at levels appropriate to their understanding.[29] All of these proposals assume that individuals will not simply debate from fixed positions, but will have access to the materials they will need to allow "enlightened preferences"[30] to emerge. Yet information alone, while necessary, is not by itself sufficient for reasoned deliberation. Two other matters also present critical barriers to the efficacious exercise of public reason: emotions and values. Emotions may involve a range of attachments, but the ones that would be most significant for our purposes here would be those that manifest as prejudices, biases, and hatred. These "afflictive emotions"[31] pose tremendous obstacles to discussions proceeding in good faith, with a fair examination of issues. It is the fear of such emotional cauldrons that makes adversary democratic procedures so appealing in the first place; we can avoid mining potentially explosive subjects by keeping our distance from one another and using procedures that shield us, such as secret ballots and majority rule. If we think there are benefits to be derived from making greater use of face-to-face discussions, participation, and deliberation in our society, we will have to provide mechanisms to safely deal with such emotional roadblocks. This may involve training for civic involvement, as well as the presence of professional facilitators who have the expertise to deal with such states of mind. Clearly, more research is needed on the effect of emotions and mental states on the capacity of citizens to effectively talk, act, and deliberate together, as they seek to uncover elements of a commonweal.[32]

Alongside of emotional attachments, and in some cases linked to them, is the issue of value commitments that may provide meaning to individuals' lives, but may pose problems as we talk about a *civil ethos*. Here again, we will have to provide procedures that allow us to distinguish between deliberative disagreements and nondeliberative disagreements. While participants may need to reference their own comprehensive belief systems[33] in order to clarify the origins of their positions, there will also have to be a willingness to move to a middle ethical ground appropriate to a diverse, multicultural society. There are three safeguards here to protect against harm to nonmajority orientations in any of these proceedings. First, the deliberations can always switch from a unitary approach to an adversary model if it becomes clear that no agreement about common concerns can be reached.[34] Second, deliberations will be advisory to the actual "will formation" of formal legislative institutions,[35] and, despite the growing fragility of linkages between elected officials and their constituents, voting still provides citizens with a prescribed measure of accountability from their representatives (which citizens may not have from the participants in the public sphere, governmental sector, and realm of civil ethics who "stand for" them in these deliberations).[36] And finally, of course, the courts will remain a significant locus for the protection of individual rights in a diverse and complex society.

The case of the Adams Center Landfill provides one model for how a deliberative process might successfully be used in an environmental dispute. Here, a policy issue that was extremely polarized and highly adversarial found a resolution through an approach that used as its beacons fairness, the public good, and a concern for the future. The members of the Indiana Hazardous Waste Facility Site Approval Authority were chosen by state and local officials to represent particular categories written into a legislative statute. They had access to a great deal of information from a variety of perspectives, including public testimony, written submissions, agency documents, and the reports of expert consultants, as well as an adjudicatory hearing, which operated along the lines of a "science court."[37] While this deliberation did not explicitly address ethics or biospheric values, the members of the Siting Authority were able to develop a broad perspective on the conflict before them, listen closely to the concerns of the various constituencies involved, gather a strong base of information, and pay careful attention to one another; these factors allowed them to eventually move toward an equitable and environmentally sound decision. The approach of the Siting Authority falls within the category of what Ben A. Minteer and Bob Pepperman Taylor discuss as "democratic pragmatism"; while not explicitly addressing "foundational" environmental values, the deliberative process, by being open to the best interests of the parties involved and with an eye to what the Siting Authority members conceived to be the commonweal, reached a more effective solution than was being produced under adversarial methods.[38] Additional research is needed to systematically evaluate a variety of deliberative approaches in order to more fully understand what mechanisms work best for what policy issues under what sets of circumstances—and what policy issues and what circumstances are not amenable to deliberative procedures—so that other, more adversarial, approaches should be considered.

The Adams Center Landfill case focused on a set of policy issues that emerged on the public policy agenda in the United States in the late 1970s and, to some extent, still remains high on the roster of what Americans consider to be significant environmental problems. Yet a growing number of experts began to argue, in the late 1980s and early 1990s, that the most critical environmental problems facing the nation and the world were not contamination threats from regional sites, but rather global dangers, such as climate change, deforestation, and the loss of biodiversity. Chapters 4 and 5 explored two issues central to those biospheric concerns: energy policies and global climate change strategies.[39] Since energy issues pervade every aspect of our existence, and since they have such profound implications for the integrity and functioning of the biosphere, they are pivotal. Energy issues involve not only resource limits, but serious pollution consequences as well. Since it is clear that fossil fuels are a finite resource, our nation would need to address other energy options, even if the use of fossil fuels weren't intimately related to global climate change. A bold orientation to these issues may require the real involvement of American citizens, first, in understanding the consequences of the different energy choices we make and, then, in helping to develop policy directions for the short-term, middle-term, and long-term planning framework.[40] If we were able to more democratically discuss and act on these issues among ourselves, we might be better able to see the consequences of our present approach and the dangers that lie ahead if we don't critically reexamine it. Deeper involvement in these issues by citizens at the local, state, and national levels might also be a precursor to a greater openness to talking, acting, setting goals, and reaching agreements with other nations on these issues. The United States has regrettably abandoned its leadership role on global environmental issues at this time, when our nation is more powerful than ever, but viewed with growing apprehension by other nations.[41] Based on a survey by the Pew

Research Center for People and the Press, conducted to assess attitudes about America in forty-four countries in December 2002, Andrew Kohut, the center's director, observed: "The main lesson is that while there is a reserve of good will toward the United States, the most powerful country in the world has an increasing number of detractors . . . old friends who need us less, like us less."[42]

This seeming lack of concern for maintaining cooperative and respectful relationships with the other nations of the world, at least by the present administration in Washington, also seems to characterize our present policy indifference toward ecosystems and other species on the earth. From a purely self-interested perspective, we should want to protect the diversity of life on the planet because we are ultimately so dependent on it for our own survival.[43] Yet beyond this, a claim could also be made about the ethical responsibility we have to take care of the other species with whom we share the biosphere. A pioneer in this field of ecology, Jane Goodall, recently commented:

> the world is changing. We are gradually becoming more aware of the damage we inflict on the natural world. This awareness is creeping into science, into the hearts and minds of the general public, and also into legislation—all around the world more laws protecting animals and the environment are passed each year. For many species, though, our new understanding has come too late—they are gone. For thousands of suffering individual animals the pace of change has been too slow, but with the introduction of new measures we are gradually replacing cruelty with compassion and creating a world in which humans can live in peace and harmony with the natural world.[44]

This view is being expressed not only by "bleeding heart liberals" (it is not at all clear that this is how Jane Goodall would describe herself), but conservative Republicans, as well. Matthew Scully, a former speechwriter for George W. Bush, author of *Dominion: The Power of Man, the Suffering of Animals, and the Call to Mercy*, wrote an op-ed piece for the *New York Times*, commenting on the implications of lifting the fourteen-year-old ban on the sale of elephant ivory, which the United States helped to initiate.

> We are talking here about intelligent mammals whose entire population was cut in half in a single decade. Even now swarms of poachers slaughter thousands of elephants every year. Such is the trauma inflicted on the herds that scientists have lately noticed a strange frequency of both African and Asian elephants born with no tusks at all. By a genetic quirk a tiny percentage of male elephants have always been tuskless. Now, as if evolution itself were trying to spare them from human avarice, that gene is spreading because the tuskless ones are often the only ones left to breed.[45]

More research may be needed to understand how Americans actually view their relationship to the natural world; how their values on this subject are shaped; what conditions might motivate them to participate in discussions, activities, and deliberations about the biosphere; what contexts enhance deliberations about a civil ethos; and what circumstances frustrate such efforts. In addition, research may be needed to better understand what Americans currently see as their role in the world, what they believe the nature of our relationship with other nations should be, and what the character of our involvement in international institutions, such as the United Nations, should be. The contemporary emphasis in American culture and in the American political ethos on individual rights may now be posing significant problems for how we choose to deal with environmental problems and how, or whether, we will enter into global discussions on this subject. The concept of sustainable development implies that humans have special responsibilities concerning how we care for the planet. Adopting such an orientation would require Americans to more seriously consider their impacts on the natural world and their obligations to each other, future generations, other species, and other nations. It would require thoughtfully and pragmatically developing a workable model of a sustainable society.[46] Americans are extremely skilled at implementing programs and taking actions when they understand the need to do so. Understanding that there is now a need to do so will depend on active and ethical citizens and thoughtful and ethical leaders. Together, we may be able to build a viable, accountable, compassionate, and principled path to the future.

NOTES

1. Robert N. Bellah, *The Broken Covenant: American Civil Religion in Time of Trial,* 2nd ed. (Chicago: University of Chicago Press, 1992); Michael Sandel, *Democracy's Discontent: America in Search of a Public Philosophy* (Cambridge: Belknap Press of Harvard University Press, 1996); Amitai Etzioni, *The New Golden Rule: Community and Morality in a Democratic Society* (New York: Basic, 1996); Martin E. Marty, *The One and the Many: America's Struggle for the Common Good* (Cambridge, Mass.: Harvard University Press, 1997); Benjamin R. Barber, *A Place for Us: How to Make Society Civil and Democracy Strong* (New York: Hill and Wang, 1998).

2. Sandel, *Democracy's Discontent,* 3–24.

3. Lisabeth Cohen, *A Consumers' Republic: The Politics of Mass Consumption in Postwar America* (New York: Knopf, 2003); David Brooks, *Bobos in Paradise: The New Upper Class and How They Got There* (New York: Simon & Schuster, 2000).

4. Sandel, *Democracy's Discontent,* 3–24.

5. Jane Mansbridge, *Beyond Adversary Democracy* (Chicago: University of Chicago Press, 1983), 299–303.

6. Robert Bellah et al., *Habits of the Heart: Individualism and Commitment in American Life* (Berkeley: University of California Press, 1985); Robert Wuthnow, *Loose Connections: Joining Together in America's Fragmented Communities* (Cambridge, Mass.: Harvard University Press, 1998); Arlie Hochschild, *The Time Bind: When Work Becomes Home and Home Becomes Work* (New York: Henry Holt, 1997).

7. Bellah, *Broken Covenant*; Sandel, *Democracy's Discontent*.

8. As noted earlier in the book, Sandel in *Democracy's Discontent* (317–352) argues that reliance on individuals to construct a purposeful moral universe courts the twin problems of "drift," where no strong moral compass emerges, and of fundamentalism, where, in response to so many choices, an individual clings to a rigid belief system.

9. Hochschild, *Time Bind*.

10. Kevin Phillips, *Wealth and Democracy: A Political History of the American Rich* (New York: Broadway, 2002); Barber, *Place for Us*, 69–113, 124–148. In 2001, 59 percent of Americans defined themselves as middle-class; the median household income was $42,228. However, 80 percent of Americans earned less than $83,500, the top 20 percent more than $83,500, and the top 5 percent of Americans earned more than $150,499; see David Leonhardt, "Defining the Rich in the World's Richest Country," *New York Times Week in Review*, 12 January 2003, 1, 16 (4). Moreover, in *Wealth and Democracy* (121), Phillips points out that in 1981, the top 1 percent of Americans commanded about 9 percent of the personal income in the United States, while in 1997, the top 1 percent commanded almost 16 percent of the personal income in America.

11. Mansbridge, *Beyond Adversary Democracy*; Sandel, *Democracy's Discontent*, 25–54, 91–122.

12. Mansbridge, *Beyond Adversary Democracy*, 3–38, 299–303.

13. Roger Fisher and William Ury, *Getting to Yes: Negotiating Agreement without Giving In* (New York: Penguin, 1991); Nancy E. Abrams and Joel R. Primack, "The Public and Technological Decisions," *Bulletin of Atomic Scientists* 6 (June 1980): 44–48.

14. See Dorothy Nelkin and Michael M. Pollack, "Public Participation in Technological Decisions: Reality or Grand Illusion?" *Technology Review* 81 (8): 55–64; William D. Ruckelshaus, "Risk in a Free Society," *Environmental Law Reporter* 14: 1090–1092; and Abrams and Primack, "The Public and Technological Decisions."

15. Robert Dahl, *Controlling Nuclear Weapons: Democracy versus Guardianship* (Syracuse: Syracuse University Press, 1985); Edward O. Wilson, *The Future of Life* (New York: Knopf, 2002); Benjamin Barber, *Strong Democracy: Participatory Politics for a New Age* (Berkeley: University of California Press, 1984); Paul Wachtel, *The Poverty of Affluence: A Psychological Portrait of the American Way of Life* (Philadelphia, Pa.: New Society, 1989).

16. Sandel, *Democracy's Discontent*, 91–122.

17. Jane J. Mansbridge, "A Deliberative Theory of Interest Representation," in *The Politics of Interests: Interest Groups Transformed*, ed. Mark P. Petracca (Boulder, Colo.: Westview, 1992), 32–57; Joshua Cohen, "Procedure and Substance in Deliberative Democracy," in *Deliberative Democracy: Essays on Reason and Politics*, ed. James Bohman and William Rehg (Cambridge, Mass.: MIT Press, 1999), 407–438.

18. Sandel, *Democracy's Discontent*, 91–122. Bernard Williams observes in his book *Truth and Truthfulness: An Essay in Genealogy* (Princeton, N.J.: Princeton University Press, 2002) that truth is developed out of the attributes of sincerity and accuracy. See also Christopher Lehmann-Haupt, "Sir Bernard Williams, 73, Oxford Philosopher Dies," *New York Times*, 14 June 2003, 28 (A).

19. Lin Yutang, ed., *The Wisdom of India and China* (New York: Random House, 1942), 811–864.

20. Fisher and Ury, *Getting to Yes*, 48.

21. Amy Gutmann and Dennis Thompson, *Democracy and Disagreement* (Cambridge, Mass.: Belknap Press of Harvard University Press, 1996), 1–10.

22. Mansbridge, *Beyond Adversary Democracy*.

23. The Dalai Lama, *Ethics for a New Millennium* (New York: Riverhead, 1999), 193–194.

24. See John Rawls, "The Idea of Public Reason," in *Deliberative Democracy*, ed. Bohman and Rehg, 93–144; Wilson, *The Future of Life*; The World Commission on Environment and Development, *Our Common Future* (New York: Oxford University Press, 1987); Jane Goodall and Marc Bekoff, *The Ten Trusts: What We Must Do to Care for the Animals We Love* (San Francisco: HarperSanFrancisco, 2002); Matthew Scully, *Dominion: The Power of Man, the Suffering of Animals, and the Call to Mercy* (New York: St. Martin's, 2002); Shierry Weber Nicholsen, *The Love of Nature and the End of the World: The Unspoken Dimensions of Environmental Concern* (Cambridge, Mass.: MIT Press, 2002).

25. See Everett Carll Ladd, *The Ladd Report* (New York: Free Press, 1999). Robert D. Putnam, in *Bowling Alone: The Collapse and Revival of American Community* (New York: Simon & Schuster, 2000), argues that there has been a significant decline in Americans' participation in civil society, yet he makes the argument that a renewed commitment to community engagement is feasible in the United States.

26. See, among others, Michael Edelstein, *Contaminated Communities: The Social and Psychological Impacts of Residential Toxic Exposure* (Boulder, Colo.: Westview, 1988); Kai Erikson, *A New Species of Trouble: Explorations in Disaster, Trauma and Community* (New York: Norton, 1994); Jonathan Harr, *A Civil Action* (New York: Vintage, 1995); Ted Bernard and Jora Young, *The Ecology of Hope: Communities Collaborate for Sustainability* (Gabriola Island, British Columbia: New Society, 1997); James E. Crowfoot and Julia M. Wondolleck, *Environmental Disputes: Community Involvement in Conflict Resolution* (Washington, D.C.: Island, 1990); and William A. Shutkin, *The Land That Could Be: Environmentalism and Democracy in the Twenty-First Century* (Cambridge, Mass.: MIT Press, 2001). See also the more general appraisals of American involvement in community issues, such as Daniel Kemmis, *Community and the Politics of Place* (Norman: University of Oklahoma Press, 1990); Craig A. Rimmerman, *The New Citizenship: Unconventional Politics, Activism, and Service* (Boulder, Colo.: Westview, 1997); and Richard C. Box, *Citizen Governance: Leading American Communities into the 21st Century* (Thousand Oaks, Calif.: Sage, 1998).

27. Allen Schnaiberg and Kenneth Alan Gould, *Environment and Society: The Enduring Conflict* (Blackburn, 2000); Juliet B. Schor, *The Overworked American: The Unexpected Decline of Leisure* (New York: Basic, 1991).

28. Herman E. Daly, *Beyond Growth* (Boston: Beacon, 1996); Todd Rakoff, *Time for Every Purpose: Law and the Balance of Life* (Cambridge, Mass.: Harvard University Press, 2002).

29. Dahl, *Controlling Nuclear Weapons*, 69–89.

30. Mansbridge, *Beyond Adversary Democracy*, 25.

31. The Dalai Lama, *Ethics for a New Millennium*. "In Tibetan, we call such negative and emotional events *nyong mong*, literally 'that which afflicts from within' or, as the term is usually translated, 'afflictive emotion.' On this view, generally speaking, all those thoughts, emotions, and mental events which reflect a negative or uncompassionate state of mind (*kun long*) inevitably undermine our experience of inner peace. All negative thoughts and emotions—such as hatred, anger, pride, lust, greed, envy, and so on—are considered to be afflictions in this sense" (86).

32. In a recent book entitled *Upheavals of Thought: The Intelligence of Emotions* (Cambridge, England: Cambridge University Press, 2001), philosopher Martha C. Nussbaum explores the relationship between emotions and ethics, particularly the positive role that emotions such as compassion and love may play.

33. John Rawls, *Justice as Fairness: A Restatement*, ed. Erin Kelly (Cambridge, Mass.: Belknap Press of Harvard University Press, 2001).

34. Mansbridge, *Beyond Adversary Democracy*.

35. Jürgen Habermas, *Between Facts and Norms: Contributions to a Discourse Theory of Law and Democracy*, trans. William Rehg (Cambridge, Mass.: MIT Press, 1996).

36. Dahl, *Controlling Nuclear Weapons*.

37. Nelkin and Pollack, "Public Participation."

38. Ben A. Minteer and Bob Pepperman Taylor, eds., *Democracy and the Claims of Nature: Critical Perspectives for a New Century* (Lanham, Md.: Rowman & Littlefield, 2002). Of course, it should be remembered that the Siting Authority was able to operate as effectively as it did partly because the contending interests in the dispute had obtained some measure of social and political parity in the surrounding community.

39. Christopher J. Bosso and Deborah Lynn Guber, "The Boundaries and Contours of American Environmental Activism," in *Environmental Policy: New Directions for the Twenty-First Century*, eds. Norman J. Vig and Michael E. Kraft (Washington, D.C.: Congressional Quarterly, 2003), 79–102.

40. G. Tyler Miller Jr., *Living in the Environment: Principles, Connections, and Solutions*, 12th ed. (Belmont, Calif.: Wadsworth, 2002), 334.

41. Adam Clymer, "World Survey Says Negative Views of U.S. Are Rising," *New York Times*, 5 December 2002, 22 (A); Michael Ignatieff, "The Burden," *New York Times Magazine*, 5 January 2003, 22; Joseph S. Nye Jr., *The Paradox of American Power: Why the World's Only Superpower Can't Go It Alone* (New York: Oxford University Press, 2002).

42. Clymer, "World Survey." This book is being completed after the United States failed to work through the United Nations to reach a diplomatic and broadly-based multi-lateral solution to the disarming of Iraq and engaged in a war that is viewed very negatively not only by Arab nations, but by many other nations around the world. See Richard Bernstein, "Press and Public Abroad Seem to Grow Ever Angrier against the U.S.," *New York Times*, 27 March 2003, 2 (B).

43. Wilson, *The Future of Life*.

44. Goodall and Bekoff, *Ten Trusts*, xvi.

45. Matthew Scully, "Don't Resume the Elephant Harvest," *New York Times*, 1 October 2002, 31 (A).

46. One recent and possibly hopeful indication that the notion of sustainability can be pragmatically addressed within the American political system was the announcement of a plan called the "Apollo Project," in which ten labor unions in the United States are supporting a research effort that would "promote energy efficiency, reduce dependence on foreign oil, and preserve manufacturing jobs." See Steven Greenhouse, "Unions Back Research Plan for Energy," *New York Times*, 6 June 2003, 20 (A).

Index

Abraham, Spencer, 78
Abrams, Nancy E., 33–34
acid rain, 76, 77, 82, 92–93
Adams Center Hazardous Waste Landfill: agriculture and, 43, 52, 60; Allen County and, 49, 61–63; Chemical Waste Management, Incorporated and, 46, 47, 48, 49, 59, 61–63; closing of, 42, 58, 61; common good and, 117–18; cultural issues of risk and, 46–47, 53; deliberation and, 3, 41, 54–56, 58–61, 62–63, 117–18; economy and, 43, 51–52, 53, 57, 60, 61–63; environment and, 47, 53, 54, 55–56, 57; experts and, 54, 55; Fort Wayne and, 47–48, 57–58, 61–63; history of, 41–52; Indiana Hazardous Waste Facility Site Approval Authority and, 42, 49–50, 51–57, 58–61, 117–18; information and, 48, 53–54, 55–56, 57, 117–18; litigation over, 48–49, 50–51, 57, 58, 59, 61; New Haven and, 47, 59, 61–63; permitting process for, 46–48, 49, 50, 59; post-closure usage of, 61–63; technical issues of risk and, 47, 54, 55, 61. See also Adams Center Sanitary Waste Landfill
Adams Center Sanitary Waste Landfill, 44–46. See also Adams Center Hazardous Waste Landfill
adversary democracy, 26, 27, 103, 110–11, 116
adversary systems: of deliberation, 30–31, 36, 60–61, 117; of democracy, 26, 27, 103, 110–11, 116
agriculture, 43, 52, 60, 69
air pollution, 76, 82, 86, 91–96, 99. See also climate change
Allen County: Adams Center Hazardous Waste Landfill and, 49, 61–63; Adams Center Sanitary Waste Landfill and, 44–45; Chemical Waste Management, Incorporated and, 60; demographics of, 42–44, 46; Indiana Hazardous Waste Facility Site Approval Authority and, 52, 53, 56; litigation against, 50–51, 59, 61; stop-work orders and, 50–51, 57
Allen County Dump Stoppers: formation of, 46; Indiana Hazardous Waste Facility Site Approval Authority and, 60; opposition work by, 48, 59; post-closure usage and, 62, 63; reparations and, 61
America (My Country 'Tis of Thee), 21
America the Beautiful, 21
Amy, Douglas, 59
Apollo Project, 124n46
Arctic National Wildlife Refuge, 79, 113
Arendt, Hannah, 4, 17, 25, 28, 29
attachment, 8, 24–25, 35, 36
awareness, 116

balance of power, 59
Barber, Benjamin, 38n29, 101, 102, 103
Bates, Katherine Lee, 21
Bayh, Evan, 60

belief systems, 6–7, 8, 22–23. *See also* religion; values
Bell, Daniel, 8
Bellah, Robert, 5–6, 18, 19
Benhabib, Seyla, 8, 9, 17–18
Berlin, Irving, 21
Bible, 5
Bill of Rights, 5. *See also* Constitution
biomass, 80–81, 85
Brandeis, Louis, 71
Brint, Steven, 7–8
Bush, George H. W., 11, 76, 97
Bush, George W., 12, 13, 77–80, 92, 98–100
business, 71

Caldwell, Lynton K., 91
Carson, Rachel, 11, 72
Carter, Jimmy, 17, 75, 78–79
Chemical Waste Management, Incorporated: Adams Center Hazardous Waste Landfill and, 46, 47, 48, 49, 59, 61–63; Adams Center Sanitary Waste Landfill and, 45–46; Allen County and, 60; Fort Wayne and, 57–58, 60; Indiana Department of Environmental Management and, 58; Indiana Hazardous Waste Facility Site Approval Authority and, 51–52, 53–54, 55–56, 56–57, 60; litigation and, 51, 57–58, 59, 61; New Haven and, 60
Cheney, Dick, 77–78
Chernobyl Reactor, 83
chlorofluorocarbons, 93–94
Christy, John, 95
civic republicanism: agriculture and, 69; consumer rights and, 71; democracy and, 101–2; discussion and, 27; economy and, 24, 71–72; exclusivity and, 5; freedom and, 5–7; New Deal and, 71; procedural liberalism and, 5–7, 8–9; sacred values and, 22
shared principles and, 4–5, 5–6
civil ethics: belief systems and, 22–23; common good and, 74–75; consensus and, 112–14; deliberation and, 22–23, 110, 114–15; democracy and, 2–3, 101, 110–11; discussion and, 23, 24, 27–28, 115; environment and, 2–3, 10, 13, 23, 101, 103–5, 109, 120; governmental sectors and, 21–23, 109–15; middle way and, 2–3, 113, 114–15; model of, 24, 27; participation and, 23, 24, 27, 28, 115; policy and, 23; public sphere and, 9–10, 21–23, 109–15; religion and, 21–23; shared principles and, 7; social contract and, 112–13; values and, 21–23, 112–13, 117
Civilian Conservation Corps (CCC), 71, 103
civil religion, 18–21. *See also* religion
civil society: attachment and, 24–25; community and, 24–25; discussion and, 9–10, 24; freedom and, 25; governmental sectors and, 17–18; model of, 24–25; participation and, 7, 9–10, 18, 24, 28; public sphere and, 9–10, 17–18, 26; religion and, 22; social capital and, 25. *See also* society
Clean Air Act
new source review program under, 99; passage of, 72, 76; pollutants under, 91, 92, 93
Clean Water Act, 72, 76
climate change: chlorofluorocarbons and, 93–94; deliberation and, 3, 100–105; discussion and, 100–105, 118; economy and, 98, 99; energy policy and, 3, 86; environment and, 93–96, 98, 99, 118; fossil fuels and, 82, 94, 97; industrialization and, 97; international conventions on, 13, 76, 77, 96–100; participation and, 100–105, 118; responsibility and, 92, 97; sustainable development and, 13; water and, 55. *See also* pollution
Clinton, Hillary R., 79
Clinton, William J., 11, 76–77, 79, 98, 99, 100
coal, 81, 82, 92–93. *See also* fossil fuels
Cohen, Joshua, 28–29

common good: Adams Center Hazardous Waste Landfill and, 117–18; civil ethics and, 74–75; deliberation and, 28–29, 30–31, 35, 36, 55, 61, 111, 117–18; democracy and, 102, 111; discussion and, 36; energy policy and, 75, 79–80; environment and, 100–101; freedom and, 8; industrialization and, 4; middle way and, 2; procedural republicanism and, 22; values and, 117. *See also* shared principles

communes, 39n62

community: agriculture and, 69; civil religion and, 18–21; civil society and, 24–25; definition of, 1; democracy and, 6; equality and, 2, 7–8; freedom and, 2, 7–8; friendship and, 19; industrialization and, 4, 69; music and, 20–21; polity and, 1–2, 3–10, 74–75, 109; sacred and, 18–19

Comprehensive Environmental Response, Compensation, and Liability Act (CERCLA), 42

conflict, 27–28, 30, 41, 103, 111

consensus, 22, 26, 30–31, 36, 55, 112–14

conservation, energy, 84, 85

conservationists, environmental, 69–70

Constitution, 5, 26–27. *See also* constitutional state

constitutional state, 9, 24, 26–27

consumer rights, 71

consumption, 116

control, 32

Convention on Biodiversity, 76

Convention on Global Climate Change, 76

cooperation, 104–5, 118–19

courts, 117

critical review and public assessment, 33–34

cultural issues of risk, 46–47, 53

Dahl, Robert, 31–32, 34, 103

Dalai Lama, 23, 115, 123n31

Declaration of Independence, 5, 19–20

deliberation: Adams Center Hazardous Waste Landfill and, 3, 41, 54–56, 58–61, 62–63, 117–18; adversary systems of, 30–31, 36, 60–61, 117; attachment and, 35, 36; balance of power and, 59; civil ethics and, 22–23, 110, 114–15; climate change and, 3, 100–105; common good and, 28–29, 30–31, 35, 36, 55, 61, 111, 117–18; conflict and, 30; consensus and, 22, 30–31, 36, 55; democracy and, 4, 31–32, 55, 87n21, 110–12; disagreements and, 113–14, 117; discussion and, 30, 31–32, 33, 34, 48, 54; economy and, 24; emotions and, 116–17; energy policy and, 79, 80, 86, 87n21, 100–105; environment and, 3, 13, 32, 100–105, 109, 113–15, 116–18, 120; equality and, 29, 31, 35, 36; experts and, 32, 33–34, 35, 111–12, 113; fossil fuels and, 113; governmental sectors and, 26, 61; Indiana Hazardous Waste Facility Site Approval Authority and, 3, 41, 54–56, 58–61, industrialization and, 4; information and, 29, 33, 34–35; juries and, 29–30; limits and, 104; middle way and, 2–3, 113; minipopulus and, 32, 103; models of, 30–34; nuclear waste and, 33–34; participation and, 31, 32, 49; policy considerations and, 34–35; prerequisites of, 29–30, 34–36, 87n21, 116; procedural liberalism and, 22; public sphere and, 9–10, 26, 31, 61, 104; purpose of, 28–29; religion and, 114; respect and, 29, 31, 55; responsibility and, 104; self-interest and, 29–30, 35, 35–36, 113, 116–17; shared principles and, 113–15; societal spheres and, 28–36; sustainable development and, 103–4; trust and, 29, 35, 36; unitary systems of, 30–31, 117; values and, 35, 117

democracy: adversary, 26, 27, 103, 110–11, 116; belief systems and, 7; civil ethics and, 2–3, 101, 110–11; common good and, 102, 111; community and, 6; conflict and, 41, 103, 111; consensus and, 26; control and, 32; deliberation and, 4, 31–32, 55, 87n21, 110–12; discussion and, 27; economy and, 24; environment and, 1, 2, 3, 101; equality and, 4; experts and, 31, 111–12; industrialization and, 4; information and, 31–32; models of, 101–2; money and, 31, 112; participation and, 87n21, 110–12; polity and, 4; pragmatism and, 118; private realm and, 111; procedural liberalism and, 102; public sphere and, 9–10; republicanism and, 101–2, 111; strong, 102; unitary systems of, 4, 55, 111; values and, 110–11

Democratic Party, 75

democratic pragmatism, 118

Dewey, John, 24, 41

disagreements, 113–14, 117

discussion: civic republicanism and, 27; civil ethics and, 23, 24, 27–28, 115; civil society and, 9–10, 24; climate change and, 100–105, 118; common good and, 36; conflict and, 27–28; constitutional state and, 9, 24, 26–27; deliberation and, 30, 31–32, 33, 34, 48, 54; democracy and, 27; emotions and, 116–17; energy policy and, 77–78, 79, 80, 86, 100–105, 118; environment and, 2, 9–10, 11, 100–105, 109, 120; freedom and, 27; friendship and, 27; governmental sectors and, 24, 26, 26–27; justice and, 10; middle way and, 2; private realm and, 110; procedural liberalism and, 7, 27; public sphere and, 6, 7, 24, 25–26; religion and, 26–27; sacred values and, 22; self-interest and, 116–17; societal spheres and, 27–28; sustainable development and, 12; values and, 26–27

Douglass, Frederick, 20

drift, 8, 25, 121n8

due process, 2, 102

Durkheim, Emile, 4, 18–19, 20

Earth Day, 73

The Earth in the Balance, 76

economy: Adams Center Hazardous Waste Landfill and, 43, 51–52, 53, 57, 60, 61–63; civic republicanism and, 24, 71–72; climate change and, 98, 99; deliberation and, 24; democracy and, 24; energy policy and, 77–79, 98, 113; environment and, 10–13, 72, 73–74, 76–77, 78–79, 98, 103–4, 113; governmental sectors and, 24; private realm and, 24; procedural republicanism and, 71–72; sustainability and, 12–13, 116. *See also* sustainable development

Edelstein, Michael, 45, 46, 47

elections, 11–12, 77, 117

elephants, 119

Elliott, Herschel, 103, 104

emotions, 116–17

Endangered Species Act, 72

energy efficiency, 84

energy policy: American history of, 80–86; Bush, George W., and, 77–80; climate change and, 3, 86; common good and, 75, 79–80; conservation and, 85; deliberation and, 79, 80, 86, 87n21, 100–105; discussion and, 77–78, 79, 80, 86, 100–105, 118; economy and, 77–79, 98, 113; efficiency and, 84, 85; environment and, 3, 68, 77, 78–79, 82–84, 85, 86, 113, 118; health and, 86; industrialization and, 68, 81; information and, 79; Kyoto Protocol and, 85; nonrenewable energy and, 81–84, 86, 91–96; participation and, 80, 86, 87n21, 100–105, 118; planning and, 68; pollution and, 68, 82, 85, 86; public sphere and, 80; renewable energy and, 80–81, 84–86; sustainable development and, 12

enlightened preference, 34, 116

environment: Adams Center Hazard-

ous Waste Landfill and, 47, 53, 54, 55–56, 57; agriculture and, 69; American history of, 68–77; awareness and, 116; business and, 71; civil ethics and, 2–3, 10, 13, 23, 101, 103–5, 109, 120; climate change and, 93–96, 98, 99, 118; common good and, 100–101; conservationists and, 69–70; cooperation and, 104–5, 118–19; deliberation and, 3, 13, 32, 100–105, 109, 113–15, 116–18, 120; democracy and, 1, 2, 3, 101; discussion and, 2, 9–10, 11, 100–105, 109, 120; economy and, 10–13, 72, 73–74, 76–77, 78–79, 98, 103–4, 113; emotions and, 116–17; energy policy and, 3, 68, 77, 78–79, 82–84, 85, 86, 113, 118; individualism and, 120; industrialization and, 11, 69–71, 72, 97; interconnectedness of, 2, 119; justice and, 10; limits and, 2, 13, 91; nonrenewable energy and, 91–96; participation and, 2, 9–10, 100–105, 109, 115–20; planning and, 67–68, 73; progressive movement and, 70–71; respect and, 119; responsibility and, 23, 104–5, 119; science and, 67; self-interest and, 119; shared principles and, 2, 10, 13; social class and, 72, 100; social movement for, 72–73, 100; society and, 23; sustainability and, 67–68; sustainable development and, 2, 3, 12–13, 120; values and, 120
environmental movement, 72–73, 100
Environmental Protection Agency (EPA), 45, 46–47, 73, 75, 99
equality: civil religion and, 19–20, 21; community and, 2, 7–8; deliberation and, 29, 31, 35, 36; democracy and, 4; equal protection, 2; polity and, 2, 7–8, 74, 110; procedural liberalism and, 102; procedural republicanism and, 5; sacred values and, 22; sustainable development and, 12–13. *See also* exclusivity

equal protection, 2. *See also* equality
European Union, 97, 98
exclusivity, 4, 5, 8. *See also* equality
experts: Adams Center Hazardous Waste Landfill and, 54, 55; deliberation and, 32, 33–34, 35, 111–12, 113; democracy and, 31, 111–12; issues of risk and, 47

fairness, 2, 102
Fisher, Roger, 35, 113
Fishkin, James S., 32–33
forests, 70, 99–100
Fort Wayne: Adams Center Hazardous Waste Landfill and, 47–48, 57–58, 61–63; Adams Center Sanitary Waste Landfill and, 44; Chemical Waste Management, Incorporated and, 57–58, 60; demographics of, 42–44, 46; Indiana Hazardous Waste Facility Site Approval Authority and, 52, 53; litigation against, 59
Fort Wayne-Allen County Economic Development Alliance, 61, 62
Fort Wayne Interdenominational Ministerial Alliance, 53, 62, 62–63
Fort Wayne Police Department, 62
fossil fuels: advantages of, 81; air pollution and, 82, 86, 91–96; climate change and, 94, 97; deliberation and, 113; finite nature of, 81–82, 118
Framework Convention on Climate Change, 97
freedom: attachment and, 8; civil religion and, 19–20, 21; civil society and, 25; common good and, 8; community and, 2, 7–8; discussion and, 27; drift and, 8, 25, 121n8; fundamentalism and, 8, 25, 121n8; polity and, 2, 5–6, 7–8; private realm and, 109; relativism and, 8; republicanism and, 5–7, 110; sacred values and, 22; social contract and, 5. *See also* individualism
friendship, 19, 27. *See also* respect; trust
fundamentalism, 8, 25, 121n8

General Accounting Office, 77–78
geothermal energy, 81
Gettysburg Address, 20
Gingrich, Newt, 11, 76
global warming. *See* climate change
God, 5, 20. *See also* religion; sacred, the
God Bless America, 21
golden mean, 113. *See also* middle way
Goodall, Jane, 119
Gore, Al, 11–12, 76–77, 98
Gottlieb, Robert, 69, 73
Gould, Kenneth Alan, 100
governmental sectors: civil ethics and, 21–23, 109–15; civil society and, 17–18; deliberation and, 26, 61; discussion and, 24, 26, 26–27; economy and, 24; model of, 24, 26; participation and, 24, 26; public sphere and, 9–10, 17–18; will formation and, 22, 26
Great Depression, 71
Greece, 4, 19, 101
greenhouse gases, 93–94, 95–96, 97–100
Guthrie, Woody, 21
Gutmann, Amy, 114

Habermas, Jurgen: on civil society, 9, 17–18; on deliberation, 9, 28, 29; duality and, 19; on public sphere, 6, 8–9, 25; society and, 24
Hall, John A., 27
hazardous waste, 33–34, 42, 45, 83
health, 79, 83, 86
health care policy, 79
Hull House, 70
hydrogen fuel, 85–86

Ignatieff, Michael, 104
incubation period, 45
Indiana, 43, 45
Indiana Department of Environmental Management (IDEM), 46–47, 49, 49–50, 58, 59
Indiana Hazardous Waste Facility Site Approval Authority: Allen County and, 52, 53, 56; Chemical Waste Management, Incorporated and, 51–

52, 53–54, 55–56, 56–57, 60; composition of, 52–53, 56–57, 60, 117; convening of, 49–50, 51–53, 59; decision of, 42, 55–57, 60–61, 117–18; deliberation and, 3, 41, 54–56, 58–61; Fort Wayne and, 52, 53; hearings of, 53–54, 59–60, 117–18; Indiana Department of Environmental Management and, 49–50, 59; litigation against, 49, 50, 57, 59; New Haven and, 52, 56–57; purpose of, 49
individualism, 5–7, 110, 120. *See also* freedom; self-interest
industrialization: climate change and, 97; common good and, 4; community and, 4, 69; deliberation and, 4; energy policy and, 68, 81; environment and, 11, 69–71, 72, 97; pollution and, 11, 92
information: Adams Center Hazardous Waste Landfill and, 48, 53–54, 55–56, 57, 117–18; deliberation and, 29, 33, 34–35; democracy and, 31–32; energy policy and, 79; participation and, 116–17
interconnectedness, 2, 8, 119
Intergovernmental Panel on Climate Change, 95, 98
Iraq, 123n42
issues of risk, 46–47, 53, 54, 55, 61

Jefferson, Thomas, 5, 69
Judicial Watch, 78
juries, 29–30
justice, 6–7, 10

Kohut, Andrew, 119
Krimsky, Sheldon, 46
Kyoto Protocol, 13, 77, 85, 97–100

Lamm, Richard, 103, 104
legislatures, 26
liberalism, 5–7, 8–9, 22, 27, 102, 110. *See also* procedural republicanism
liberty. *See* freedom
limits, 2–3, 13, 91, 104
Lincoln, Abraham, 20–21, 101

Lindholm, Charles, 27
Locke, John, 5
Lovins, Amory, 78, 84

Madison, James, 5
managed scarcity, 11, 77
Mansbridge, Jane: on adversary
    democracy, 26, 27, 111; on commu-
    nes, 39n62; on conflict, 30; on delib-
    eration, 30–31, 55; on enlightened
    preference, 34; on friendship, 19
manure, 85
Martin, John Bartlow, 43
Marty, Martin, 5, 74
Merton, Robert K., 28
middle way, 2–3, 8–10, 13, 113, 114–15,
    117
Miller, G. Tyler, 86
minipopulus, 32, 103
Minteer, Ben A., 118
Molina, Mario, 93
money, 31, 112
Montesquieu, Baron de, 5, 19
Montreal Protocol, 93
morality, 2–3, 6–7. *See also* belief sys-
    tems; religion; values
Muir, John, 69–70
music, 20–21

Nader, Ralph, 77
National Academy of Sciences, 98
National Environmental Policy Act
    (NEPA), 72–73
National Forest Service, 70, 100
National Oceanic and Atmospheric
    Administration, 95
National Park Service, 70
natural gas, 81, 82. *See also* fossil fuels
New Deal, 71
New Haven: Adams Center Hazardous
    Waste Landfill and, 47, 59, 61–63;
    Chemical Waste Management,
    Incorporated and, 60; demographics
    of, 43–44, 46; Indiana Hazardous
    Waste Facility Site Approval
    Authority and, 52, 56–57; litigation
    by, 48–49, 50–51, 57, 59, 61

nihilism, 8
Nixon, Richard M., 74, 75
nondeliberative disagreements, 114,
    117
nonrenewable energy, 81–84, 86, 91–96
nuclear energy, 81, 82–84
nuclear waste, 33–34, 83
Nuclear Waste Policy Act, 83

oil, 81–82, 113. *See also* fossil fuels
openness, 2
opinion formation, 22, 25
Our Common Future, 12, 96, 109
ozone layer, 93–94

Parmesan, Camille, 94–95
participation: civil ethics and, 23, 24,
    27, 28, 115; civil society and, 7, 9–10,
    18, 24, 28; climate change and, 100–
    105, 118; constitutional state and, 24,
    26–27; deliberation and, 31, 32, 49;
    democracy and, 87n21, 110–12;
    emotions and, 116–17; energy policy
    and, 80, 86, 87n21, 100–105, 118;
    environment and, 2, 9–10, 100–105,
    109, 115–20; governmental sectors
    and, 24, 26; information and,
    116–17; middle way and, 2; private
    realm and, 110; public sphere and,
    24, 26; self-interest and, 116–17;
    societal spheres and, 28; sustainable
    development and, 102, 116
Pew Research Center for People and
    the Press, 118–19
Pinchot, Gifford, 70
planning, 67–68, 73
Plough, Alonzo, 46
pluralism, 6
policy, 23, 26, 34–35. *See also* energy
    policy; health care policy
polity: common good and, 2; commu-
    nity and, 1–2, 3–10, 74–75, 109;
    democracy and, 4; equality and, 2,
    7–8, 74, 110; exclusivity and, 4, 5;
    freedom and, 2, 5–6, 7–8; friendship
    and, 19; industrialization and, 4;
    procedural liberalism and, 110; pub-

lic sphere and, 8–10; republicanism and, 4–7; values and, 74–75

pollution: air, 76, 82, 86, 91–96, 99; biomass and, 85; energy policy and, 68; environmental movement and, 73; Environmental Protection Agency and, 73, 75; industrialization and, 11, 92; nonrenewable energy and, 82, 86; progressive movement and, 69–71; social class and, 70–71, 72; sustainable development and, 13. *See also* climate change

Powell, Colin, 104

pragmatism, 118

preservationists, 69–70

Primack, Joel R., 33–34

private realm: belief systems and, 7; democracy and, 111; discussion and, 110; economy and, 24; freedom and, 109; model of, 24; participation and, 110; public sphere and, 10, 17–18, 25–26; religion and, 22

procedural liberalism, 5–7, 8–9, 22, 27, 102, 110. *See also* procedural republicanism

procedural republicanism, 4, 5–7, 8–9, 22, 71–72, 110. *See also* procedural liberalism

progressive movement, 69–71

public assessment, critical review and, 33–34

Public Health Service, 70

public reasoning, 22

public sphere: belief systems and, 6–7; civil ethics and, 9–10, 21–23, 109–15; civil society and, 9–10, 17–18, 26; deliberation and, 9–10, 26, 31, 61, 104; democracy and, 9–10; discussion and, 6, 7, 24, 25–26; energy policy and, 80; governmental sectors and, 9–10, 17–18; middle way and, 8–10; model of, 24, 25–26; morality and, 6–7; opinion formation and, 22, 25; participation and, 24, 26; polity and, 8–10; private realm and, 10, 17–18, 25–26; shared principles and, 6–7, 9–10

Purdue University, 52

Putnam, Robert D., 7, 25, 122n25

Quakers, 30

Rawls, John: on belief systems, 7; on deliberation, 9, 29, 35; on justice, 10; on public reasoning, 22; on reasonable pluralism, 6; society and, 24

Reagan, Ronald, 11, 73–74, 75–76, 77, 92

reasonable pluralism, 6

relativism, 8

religion, 18–23, 26–27, 114. *See also* belief systems; God; morality

renewable energy, 80–81, 84–86

republicanism: civic, 4–5, 5–7, 8–9, 22, 24, 27, 69, 71–72, 101–2; civil religion and, 19–21; consumer rights and, 71; democracy and, 101–2, 111; equality and, 5; freedom and, 5–7, 110; individualism and, 5–7; polity and, 4–7; procedural, 4, 5–7, 8–9, 22, 71–72, 110; self-interest and, 19; shared principles and, 4–5, 5–6

Republican Party, 74–75

Resource Conservation and Recovery Act (RCRA), 42, 45, 61, 72

respect, 29, 31, 55, 119. *See also* friendship; trust

responsibility, 23, 92, 97, 104–5, 119

Reynolds, Michael, 85

Roland, Sherwood, 93

Roosevelt, Franklin Delano, 6, 71, 101

Roosevelt, Theodore, 70, 71

Rose, Reginald, 29

sacred, the, 18–19, 21–23. *See also* God; religion

Sandel, Michael: on belief systems, 7; on consensus, 22; on freedom, 8, 25, 121n8; on republicanism, 4, 5

Sanitation Corporation of America (SCA), 45

Schlesinger, Arthur, Jr., 101

Schnaiberg, Allan, 10, 11, 12, 72, 77, 100

Schor, Juliet B., 102

science, 67
scientific mediation, 34
Scully, Matthew, 119
self-interest: common good and, 2; deliberation and, 29–30, 35, 35–36, 113, 116–17; discussion and, 116–17; environment and, 119; participation and, 116–17; republicanism and, 19. *See also* individualism
Selznick, Philip, 87n21
shared principles: civil ethics and, 7; civil religion and, 18–21; common good and, 2; deliberation and, 113–15; environment and, 2, 10, 13; industrialization and, 4; justice and, 6–7; music and, 20–21; public sphere and, 6–7, 9–10; republicanism and, 4–5, 5–6. *See also* common good
Sierra Club, 70
Silent Spring, 11, 72
Smith, Samuel Francis, 21
smog, 92. *See also* pollution
social capital, 25
social class, 70–71, 72, 100, 121n10
social contract, 5, 6, 112–13
social movements, 69–71, 72, 73, 100
society, 23–36. *See also* civil society
Soil Conservation Service, 71
solar energy, 80, 81, 84–85
solid waste, 42
songs, 20–21
Strong Democracy, 101
strong democracy, 102
Sununu, John, 76
Superfund, 42
sustainability, 67–68, 116. *See also* sustainable development
sustainable development: climate change and, 13; deliberation and, 103–4; discussion and, 12; economy and, 12–13; energy policy and, 12; environment and, 2, 3, 12–13, 120; equality and, 12–13; Gore, Al, and, 77; middle way and, 13; participation and, 102, 116. *See also* economy; sustainability

Taylor, Bob Pepperman, 118
technical issues of risk, 47, 54, 55, 61
Tennessee Valley Authority (TVA), 71
This Land Is Your Land, 21
Thompson, Dennis, 114
Thoreau, Henry David, 70
Three Mile Island Nuclear Power Plant, 83
Tocqueville, Alexis de, 9, 18
totalists, 74
Treaty of Rome, 97
tribalists, 74
trust, 29, 35, 36. *See also* friendship; respect
Twelve Angry Men, 29–30

unitary systems, 4, 30–31, 55, 111, 117
United Auto Workers, 52
United Nations, 68, 76, 95, 96–97, 99
United States, 68–86, 98–100, 104–5, 118–19. See also *specific officials*
uranium, 83, 89n74
Ury, William, 35, 113

values: civil ethics and, 21–23, 112–13, 117; civil religion and, 18–21; common good and, 117; deliberation and, 35, 117; democracy and, 110–11; discussion and, 26–27; environment and, 120; middle way and, 117; polity and, 74–75; procedural liberalism and, 102. *See also* belief systems; morality; religion
voting, 11–12, 77, 117

Washington, George, 101
Waste Management, Incorporated, 46, 47
water, 11, 55, 80–81, 85
wealth, 121n10. *See also* social class
Westbrook, Robert, 24
Whitman, Walt, 1
will formation, 22, 26, 117
Williams, Bernard, 122n18
Wilson, Edward O., 23, 67, 94

wind, 80–81, 85
wood, 80–81, 85
work, 110, 116
World Commission on Environment
  and Development, 12, 68, 96–97, 109
World Meteorological Organization, 95

World Summit on Sustainable Development, 104
Wuthnow, Robert, 7

Yucca Mountain, 83

About the Author

Jane A. Grant is associate professor of public and environmental affairs at Indiana University–Purdue University, Fort Wayne. Her research focuses on increasing citizen involvement in policy, particularly in environmental matters, making policy processes more accountable, effective, and democratic. It also focuses on developing the means to consider and act on a civil ethics in American society, one that respects the nation's concern with individualism and freedom, yet honors the search to uncover common interests, act on shared concerns, and deliberate about public values for national and global issues.